A

The Angels' Guide to Ascension

Sue Frederick

Frederick Malowany Publishing

Contents

Introduction

In the year 2023 I was doing client sessions as I've done every day for more than 20 years, helping clients connect to their guides, departed loved ones, and higher selves. Suddenly, a complete outline of an angel appeared on my wall. It was made of light. It was profound. It stayed for at least 30 minutes, allowing me to talk to it, observe it, and confirm that what I was seeing was real.

The angel told me she was my mother in the angelic realm, and that I needed to understand the angels were here to help.

Fast forward to the spring of the following year—I was diagnosed with a serious illness, and underwent major, life-threatening surgery. But in the midst of that trauma, the angels surrounded me. I could feel them. I knew they were with me. This experience opened my heart to a deeper truth: of all the divine beings in the higher realms, angels are the most accessible. They are always with us.

Are we all struggling during this time on Earth? Yes. Consciousness is accelerating at a rate never before seen in human evolution, and we are feeling the effects. Every emotion is intensified. Every busy thought is even more overwhelming. And the choice is now: will we remain stuck in our misled human minds—or will we rise into our hearts and higher selves?

We are here for one divine purpose: to love one another.

Jesus said it plainly in the Sermon on the Mount: "I give you a new commandment. It is more important than all the rest—love one another." Yet humans have been misled—by dogma, fear, and the belief in a punishing God. We've been taught we are unworthy, sinful, and small. But our souls, our hearts, have always known better.

You are a divine being. A perfect being of light and love. You chose this earthly journey. You temporarily took on a human body, a personality, a mind—just for this trip. But none of those things are your essence. They are your vehicle in this dense and heavy realm called Earth, where your purpose is to grow, open your heart, quiet your mind, and help others.

And yet, we forget. We're talked out of who we are from childhood. By the time we remember, we've often walked through so much fear, doubt, and suffering that we've forgotten our original purpose. We live in fear: of money, of heartbreak, of loss. What a waste of a sacred life.

When we die, the angels are there. They lift us up in love, review our lives without judgment, and show us that all we had to do was love courageously, live with passion, follow our gifts, and choose kindness over fear.

So I ask you: how are you doing here on Earth?

Has the density of this realm dimmed your ability to love? Is your time spent in anxiety, fear, and self-doubt? If so, you are not alone. Most humans are experiencing this consciousness shift as a time of isolation, confusion, anger, and fear.

But now—it's time to Angel Up.

That means remembering that the God Source is all-loving, ever-present, and flowing through you at every moment. Your mind may block your ability to feel it. But your heart knows. Your soul remembers.

You have spirit guides who've loved you since your soul first sparked into being. They approved your life plan—all the challenges, all the gifts—so you could wake up. So you could Angel Up. So you could remember you are a higher being having a temporary human experience.

The angels are saying: "We are here. We have always been here. This is our only job. Let us help you. We are aiding your ascension."

In your hardest moments, have you asked for help? Have you said: "Angels, lift me up. Help me see this differently. Open my heart"? That simple prayer is all you need. It is the fastest way to feel the angels' love and presence.

Look for them. You may see them as light in a room or a photo. Your mind will say it's a glitch. But what if it's not? What if that is the angel breaking through your cynicism?

The mind is just your survival mechanism. You needed it for Earth—but you were meant to lead with your soul. With your unstoppable light.

When angels help, they don't judge. They don't counsel or analyze. They just love. They wrap you in divine light and lift you out of your pain.

You may dismiss their presence because it feels so easy, so loving. You may have been taught that being afraid, anxious, and serious means you're growing up. But the opposite is true. Your childlike joy, giggles, faith, and wonder—that was always the real you.

So now begins the deprogramming.

Each morning, ask: "Angels, lift me up today. Help me remember what I came here to do. Help me feel so loved that I radiate love to everyone I meet. Help me awaken to my own Angelic essence."

The angels are thrilled to do this with you. They are Earth's first responders.

Yes, you will have challenges. You signed up for them. But you also signed up for help—from angels, guides, and departed loved ones. They are still with you. They are proud of you.

How much of this divine support are you accessing?

In my life, when I've listened to the higher voice—even in my darkest hours—I've always found my way. My first husband died of cancer when I was 29. My best childhood friend died at 31. My soulmate friend Marv crossed in my thirties. My beloved father—my person—has crossed too. And all of them came back to tell me: "It's not what it seems. You are meant to live to the light."

Look around. Read the headlines. There is no doubt we are in a moment of great turmoil. But we are also at a choice point.

Will you listen to the voice of fear, or the voice of angels?

Cynicism may have helped you survive. But has it helped your soul thrive?

I've guided thousands of clients into the higher realms to meet their angels, their guides, their departed. And every one of them says: "I didn't believe it until now. Now I remember. That's my true home. This earth life is the dream."

In this book, I will teach you how to shift into that higher view, into your angelic ascendency while still walking the earth. We will take the steps together. You are ready now because the pain is too great to keep repeating the old patterns. As a collective, we are sick of being poisoned by hatred, fear and division. We are ready to remember love.

There is only unconditional love in the heavenly realms. And now, you are going to remember that this is the only truth; you are a being of unconditional love.

You will learn to meditate, to quiet your mind, and let your heart chakra lead you. Because your heart is the most powerful part of you.

Your mind is just a temporary transmitter of fear and judgment needed for Earth survival. Now, it's time to let your heart lead.

When your final breath comes, and you rise into the arms of the angels, you will say:

"Thank God I loved. Thank God I didn't waste my life in fear and greed. I chose light. I opened my heart. I followed my angelic intuition. I'm proud of how I lived."

And when you've ascended to the higher realms, you will help others—just as the angels helped you.

And so it is.

A Channeled Message from The Angels

Beloved one,

Things have changed on earth and we need you to understand this. We've been given a new earthly assignment for these times: To help you ascend into your true essence; to accelerate your awakening as a being of divine light - while still living your human life.

We have always been perfectly designed to save humanity from chaos. We, as a collective of Angelic Realm souls, are more formidable and stronger than the forces of hatred and division on earth.

However, at this time, we've been called up by the God Source to step into the earthly realms in more visible and accessible ways for humans; to become the most powerful divine beings on earth. To aid your ascension by lifting you into new levels of soul awakening.

Our intercession is your salvation.

You as awakened humans on earth are being asked to line up with us. To stand beside us. To engage your own angelic soul abilities and become one with us - the angelic realm team here on earth. Together we are more powerful than the darkness.

Our love will heal the chaos. We are needed. You are needed.

You are being asked to walk into every situation with the light of heaven around you like a cloak. Your sword is the cutting edge of precise unconditional love - wielded into every battle on earth. You are no longer simply human. You are now an Angel on Earth. Angel Up!

And so it is.

Chapter One

The Soul Lens

In my late twenties, I met the man of my dreams. He was beautiful, kind, intelligent—and so deeply wise. We were both mountain climbers. It was the 1970s, and we were living in Colorado, leading groups through the mountains, teaching people how to overcome fear, work together, and step into their highest and best selves. Everyone loved talking to Paul. His answers were always kind, compassionate, and—though I see it clearly now—full of angel wisdom.

Yes, Paul was a soul from the angelic realms.

He came into this lifetime briefly, offering his love, compassion, wisdom, and insight. He helped many people—as a counselor, as a mountain guide, and as a radiant soul. And I was blessed to be loved by him. We got married in a sweet little mountain chapel called the Chapel of the Pines. It seemed like the perfect life I had always dreamed of.

But then came my greatest soul challenge.

Paul was diagnosed with colon cancer at a very young age. The doctors misdiagnosed his symptoms for months. By the time they realized what it was, they gave him two weeks to live. That moment launched me onto my spiritual journey. Grief, the divine teacher, became my constant companion as we spent a year walking through Paul's suffering—trying every possible treatment, holding onto hope, praying for a miracle.

By the time Paul crossed into the light, he had become an angel of pure love. Physical suffering had purified him. He radiated courage and compassion to everyone around him. He was, without question, an ascended being.

This experience—at the age of 29—opened my eyes. I began to understand that we have two ways of seeing life. One is through the ordinary human lens, which I call the ego view. From that perspective, life is unpredictable, painful, and never quite satisfying. Every dream comes with a glitch. Every great love has a challenge. Every career ends. Eventually, we're brought to our knees by life's unexpected losses. And in those moments, we must ask ourselves the deeper questions:

Who am I, really? Why did I come here? What is my soul's purpose in the face of this heartbreak?

When we begin asking those questions, the Angels step in...

They lift us up into the soul's perspective—a view beyond the human story. We are not physical beings having a spiritual experience. We are divine souls walking through a brief human journey. Our mission here is to wake up to that truth. To recognize that everything, even our suffering, is meant to open us, transform us, and help us evolve.

As we begin to embrace this higher view, life becomes easier. The angels become more visible. Our prayers shift from "Please fix this for me" to "Please show me the blessing in this." And the angels respond—immediately, lovingly, and always in alignment with our soul's highest good.

They dry our tears. They shine light on our next step forward. They lift our hearts with laughter, a song, a moment of grace. But ultimately, we must choose to say yes to their help. Often, we stay stuck in fear, grief, or anger—unwilling to look up. But eventually, the pain becomes too much. We reach a breaking point, and we whisper a prayer:

"Angels, help me."

And they do.

During Paul's final days, little miracles occurred constantly. Visions, feelings, signs. I would be lifted out of despair and shown, for just a moment, that everything was unfolding exactly as it should. I knew Paul was already an angel, and I was being invited to learn from him in his final hours.

On the day he crossed over, I had fallen asleep on the hospital floor beside him. He appeared vividly to me, saying, "I'm ready now. I'm not trapped in this body. Please hold me so I can go." I did. I held him as his soul rose into the light. It was the most sacred moment of my life to witness his soul's ascension.

That night—and many nights after—Paul returned to show me the angelic realms. He brought visions that shattered my grief and expanded my soul. He showed me that nothing here is random or cruel. It is all on purpose. Every heartbreak is a teacher. Every loss, a portal to divine truth. Every challenge, a chance to rise.

When you hit your greatest moment of pain, try this simple prayer:

"Angels, please lift me out of this pain. Show me the light. Show me my next step forward in love."

These are the most effective prayers. The angels are always with us. They want to help—but they can't interfere until we're ready to ask. So ask.

Another way to rise out of the human story is through gratitude. In your darkest moment, ask, "What am I grateful for right now?" Maybe it's the sunshine. A warm cup of tea. Your cat curled beside you. The absence of pain in your body. Anything will do. Gratitude lifts your frequency instantly and opens your soul to divine guidance.

And then—meditate.

I've taught meditation since the 1970s. Every tradition teaches us the same truth: we are not our thoughts. Our thoughts are the byproduct of a hyper-fearful human mind designed primarily to keep us alive. We are the awareness behind those thoughts.

One of the most effective tools I've found is to repeat a sacred sound. My favorite is the Sanskrit mantra: Om Namah Shivaya.

Close your eyes. Repeat it softly inside yourself. Your mind will jump in with a distraction: "This is stupid. Do the laundry." Just notice your thoughts and say, "Thanks for your input, mind. But I'm focusing on the mantra." Gently refocus your attention to the mantra.

After 20 minutes, you'll feel it: the quiet. The light. The angelic presence. You'll see through divine eyes again.

Angelic wisdom comes to us in many forms. I remember being in my early 30s, and people would say, "What a tragedy about your husband." But I would hear the angels whisper, "Tell them it's not a tragedy." And I would gently say, "This was my greatest blessing. My spiritual awakening."

Look around your life today. Whether you're rebuilding after loss, healing a health crisis, or reinventing your work, people around you may say, "What a tragedy." Don't let that in. Say, "This is my soul's invitation to rise."

Now, more than 40 years later, I look back at Paul's early crossing as the most sacred, transformational moment of my life. Without that grief, I would not have become the soul-guided teacher I am today.

Thank you, Paul. Thank you, angels.

And blessings to your greatest spiritual teacher—whomever broke your heart open to the light.

The Om Namah Shivaya Meditation:

Step 1: Prop yourself up so that your head is not leaning back on anything or you will fall asleep. Set your timer for 20 minutes to ring in chimes and then silence your phone and put it away.

Step 2: Close your eyes and tell yourself you're not getting up for 20 minutes until the chime rings - no matter how you think this is going.

Step 3: Begin repeating the mantra Om Namah Shivaya. Repeat it silently to yourself.

Step 4: When your thoughts jump in to distract you, gently observe those thoughts. Thank your mind for sending you those thoughts. Gently refocus your attention back to the mantra. Be gentle. Don't judge yourself. Allow it to go how it goes.

Step 5: After 20 minutes open your eyes and notice how you feel. If you feel inspired to do so, pick up your pen and ask the angels for guidance. Write what you receive quickly and without editing. Let it flow.

Chapter One Summary – The Soul Lens: Seeing Beyond the Human Story

- There are two ways of seeing life: - The human lens (ego-based): sees suffering, disappointment, and danger. - The soul lens (divine perspective): sees purpose, growth, and transformation in every challenge.

- When we shift to the soul lens: - We begin to ask higher questions: Why am I here? What is my purpose? - The angels respond—lifting us, loving us, and guiding us forward.

- Prayers evolve from begging for solutions to asking for wisdom and grace within the challenge.
- The angels communicate through: - Subtle signs, laughter, sudden ideas, new connections, and peaceful knowingness even in the midst of heartbreak. - But we must be open to receive and say yes to divine help.
- Gratitude is a powerful spiritual tool: - Focusing on even small blessings can shift our vibration upward.
- Meditation quiets the ego mind and opens the soul to divine messages: - Repeating sacred mantras (e.g., Om Namah Shivaya) can help dissolve negative thoughts.
- Divine wisdom often contradicts the world's view: - What others call "tragedy" can actually be the soul's greatest initiation into awakening.
- Final reminder: When you're in pain, pray: - "Angels, please lift me. Show me my next step into the light."
- Remember, you are never alone. Help is always with you.

A Channeled Message from The Angels

Beloved One,

We are standing beside you always. We see your struggles, heartbreak and doubt. We love your courage, your endless seeking of connection and purpose, your ability to try and try again.

Take a breath. Picture a circle of us - loving beings of light - surrounding you. Relax into our presence. Let us hold you up. See the light of God's love pouring into you through us. Allow it.

Know that with every breath you take we are with you, holding you up, restoring you, loving you.

With our support, your viewpoint easily shifts. You see the miracles that have lifted you and moved you forward every moment of your lifetime – even when you felt completely abandoned and broken.

See the miracle we're handing you right now. Trust that it's real and provides the divine support you're looking for. Relax into it.

Trust this view of your life through the soul's lens. It's the real view. The real you. Always loved. Always surrounded in light. As powerful as the Angels standing beside you. And so it is.

Chapter Two

You are Never Alone

From the time I was very little, I was aware of divine beings around me—and around everyone. I saw light. I saw the Divine Mother Mary. Angels appeared in my dreams. That divine world felt more real to me than the physical world.

As I grew older, I learned how to ground myself more firmly in this physical life. I accepted that I had to live fully here and now. But the angels never left me. They were part of my daily prayers, woven into my devotion to Mother Mary. I loved the Catholic hymn that called her the Queen of Angels—that always made sense to me. That was how I understood God-consciousness as a child.

Over the years, I came to realize there are many layers of divine beings—each here to help humanity evolve. At the core is the God Source. Different religions give it different names, but it is the same: a vast, infinite consciousness of divine, unconditional love. It is not a person – though it may take that form to comfort you. It is a radiant force that creates the divine order of this universe and flows through each of us.

When we are struggling or in pain, the God Source can feel distant - even though you are part of this loving God essence and never separate from it. Our human mind deceives us; makes us feel separate.

Our departed loved ones reach out to comfort us whenever we need them. They send us signs in dreams and daily life, appearing to us in the form we remember—young, healthy, vibrant—so we will recognize them. Even if they crossed decades ago, their spirit is eternal and time is not linear. They are part of our Soul Posse so they are still with us even as they ascend into higher realms of existence.

In my life, I've had many visitations from departed loved ones: My husband Paul, who crossed in 1980; my best friend Crissie who passed a few years later, and my father, who has always been an angel guiding me. They each illuminated my life with a Shared Death Experience when they crossed – a lifting into the divine to show me the vibrant loving frequency of the realms beyond the physical world.

Many of us rely on our spirit guides for wisdom and counsel. These are powerful advisors who help us understand our soul's purpose, co-create our life plans, and navigate soul agreements. But there is another source of divine help that is often overlooked, dismissed, or misunderstood—and that is the Angelic Realm.

Here is what I want you to know: Angels are your closest allies, your first responders, and your most powerful healers. They respond instantly with light, grace, and love the moment you ask. If you're unable to ask, they simply arrive to lift you into the flow of loving grace and wisdom.

If you were raised to think angels were only for children or fairy tales, please let that image go. Right now, close your eyes and feel them.

They are light beings—sometimes formless, sometimes radiant with wings, but always a loving presence. They exist to comfort us.

All beings in the divine realms know that incarnating on Earth is one of the most challenging assignments a soul can take. Earth school is not for the faint of heart.

So the angels surround us—waiting to help.

But they cannot interfere without our invitation (except in emergency situations when it's clear to the higher realms that we need assistance).

Let this prayer be one you say often:

"Beautiful angels, please love me, heal me, help me, lift me above my pain."

They always respond.

Over the years, I've learned to recognize their voices. For me, their messages come as a high-frequency, loving collective voice. I can channel them most clearly when I write. And you can too. Quiet your mind. Breathe deeply. Pick up your pen. Let the words of love and light pour through you.

Many of my books were channeled this way. In fact, the last four books I wrote came directly from this angelic voice. I would feel so uplifted writing those books that I dreaded finishing—because I didn't want to stop hearing the angels. But now I know I don't need to be writing a book to hear them. I simply need to be still, close my eyes, and ask. They are always with us.

Years ago, I trained in soul regression therapy with Dr. Linda Backman. She helped me discover that my soul originates in the angelic realm. That revelation explained my childhood experiences—precognitive dreams, visions, and a constant connection to higher beings. This is one of my first incarnations on Earth. I came here to help humanity evolve—and to evolve my own soul in the process.

I came here to remember that I'm an Angel walking on earth - and to help you remember that you're an Angel.

I designed a lifetime that would build strength—inner and outer. Today I stand firmly on Earth, grounded in this physical realm, while still walking hand-in-hand with the angelic realms. I listen to them. I see them. I feel their love everywhere I go.

I ask you to trust the Angels. When you feel lifted, when you have a sudden knowing, a moment of peaceful empowerment in the midst of chaos—that's the angels. That's divine help reaching you.

You are never alone.

Think back to the hardest moments of your life—those heartbreaks that made you feel unloved or unworthy. I promise you: the angels were there. Loving you. Whispering to you. Singing to you. Maybe you didn't hear them. But they were holding you the entire time.

They still are.

The more you give your attention to their love and guidance, and less attention to your fearful human mind, the more your life will shift into the light. Your relationships will heal. Your health will improve. You will rise into your soul's highest potential. I've seen this in my own life and in the lives of my clients.

Let me share a few angel stories...

When I was a rock climber in my 20s, I often climbed on rock faces beyond my ability as I tried to improve my skills. There were no rock gyms so we climbed walls of extreme heights and difficulty like Eldorado Canyon in Boulder, Colorado.

One day I was leading a challenging pitch and had gone several feet without placing protection. Suddenly my foot slipped and I began careening towards the bottom of the canyon. I felt my soul leave my body and had a vision of an angel handing me a rope. My fall came to an abrupt stop.

As I regained my composure and looked up at the wall, I saw that my rope had impossibly wrapped itself around a rock outcropping and that had saved me. I heard the angels whispering to me. Their message took a long time to become clear to me. They told me to live differently that I had an important purpose and I needed to fulfill it. That moment marked the beginning of a new and better chapter for me. I still climbed but I went back to school to become a writer and pursued my soul's purpose.

Another time, when I was caring for Paul near the end of his life, I was alone and exhausted. I prayed, "God, please help him. End his suffering." Suddenly, the apartment filled with light. Paul opened his eyes and said, "Come lay beside me. Let me hold you." For hours, he was at peace—no pain, no struggle. The angels had given us that sacred time together.

Most recently, when I was diagnosed with colon cancer, I was alone in the hospital awaiting surgery. I wasn't praying in the usual way. I simply surrendered to be lifted into the wisdom of higher understanding:

"Angels, show me the way through this. Lift me up. I surrender to your wisdom."

Light filled the corners of my hospital room. The next nurse who walked in had my father's name. Later, a technician appeared with Paul's name on his badge. I knew the angels were with me, giving me strength.

The surgery was successful. Though the doctors feared the cancer had spread, it hadn't. The surgeon called it a miracle. I call it angelic intervention.

They let me stay a little longer—so I could write this for you.

Now, I invite you into a sacred experience:

A Guided Meditation to Meet Your Angels

Close your eyes. Take three deep breaths.

Inhale deeply… one… two… three…

Feel the golden light of God's unconditional love pouring down through the top of your head. It obliterates fear, clears doubt, and fills every cell of your body with vibrating love. It realigns you with your higher soul.

It prepares you for ascension.

See the golden staircase before you. It rises into the heavenly realms. Begin to climb—one step at a time.

One… two… three… four… five… six… seven… eight… nine… ten…

Walk through the tunnel of light – where all earthly pain and trauma is released. At the end of the tunnel your primary angel awaits in the light. Radiant with love.

You are embraced.

More angels appear, surrounding you with divine grace. They are singing to you. Holding you. Healing you. You feel safe. You feel deeply loved and nurtured – more than you ever have experienced on earth.

Rest here. Let them fill you with light.

Ask your questions now:

"What is mine to do next?"

"Can you heal this pain?"

"Can you guide my purpose?"

Let them work on your heart, your life, your soul.

Stay here as long as you like. Listen and receive.

When you're ready, thank the angels. Tell them you'll remember this is real.

Turn back through the tunnel…

Ten... nine... eight... seven... six... five... four... three... two... one...

Down the stairs of light back into your human body ... ten... nine... eight... seven... six... five... four... three... two... one...

Breathe deeply into your body. Feel your feet on the ground. Wiggle your fingers. Open your eyes.

Go forward into your day—surrounded by the angels who are always with you. Aware of their presence. Trusting that the invisible realms are more real than this physical world.

You are never alone.

And so it is.

Chapter Two Summary – Meeting the Angels

- The God Source is an all present, all powerful force of unconditional love; a higher consciousness that runs the universe; a divine energy that flows through all things and all people on earth – including YOU. To comfort you, this source of divine consciousness may take a form you recognize in your religious beliefs as God.

- When we're suffering, the God Source can feel distant because our human mind blocks our perception of divine truth: - Our departed loved ones often become spiritual responders—appearing in familiar forms to comfort and guide us. - Spirit guides also assist us by giving insight into life purpose, lessons, and soul agreements.

- The Angelic Realm is the most accessible, loving, and powerful support—and often the most overlooked.

- Angels are: - Our first responders. - Powerful beings of pure light and love. - Always with us but cannot interfere unless invited (except in emergencies when they can step in as needed).

- Simple and powerful angelic prayer: - "Beautiful Angels, please love me, heal me, help me, lift me above my pain."

- Anyone can channel the angels through writing: - Anyone can do this with a quiet mind, deep breathing, and intention. - Several of my books were directly channeled from the Angelic collective.

- Signs of Angelic guidance: - Feeling uplifted in dark moments and times of danger. - Receiving intuitive knowledge or grace. - Experiencing synchronicities (e.g., names of loved ones appearing in unexpected places).

- Guided Meditation Highlights: - Visualize golden light pouring through your body. - Climb 10 golden stairs into the heavenly realm. - Move through a tunnel of light to meet your primary angel. - Receive healing, love, and answers to your soul's deepest questions. - Return to Earth carrying divine wisdom and angelic support.

- Core message: - You are never alone. - The Angels are always with you—ready to heal, guide, and love you.

- You are being called to Angel Up at this time of ascension on earth; to remember that you are a being of light more powerful than any darkness.

A Channeled Message from The Angels

Beloved One,

Today when you feel alone, abandoned, heartbroken or afraid – close your eyes. Take three deep breaths. Call on us.

Say: "Angels lift me, love me, heal me."

As you cry, repeat those words quietly in your heart. Our answer is immediate. We wrap you in unconditional love, remove your pain, and lift your soul to the higher realms for healing - even as your human self stays in the earth realm. We have part of you with us – traveling through time and space to bask in God's unconditional love.

Suddenly you feel a bit lighter, a bit calmer, and an idea comes to you that brightens your heart – a friend to call or an idea that would help you move forward. It sparks you. Lifts you up – shifts your frequency into the light. You remember your Angelic power – greater than any challenge that comes your way.

This is our job. This is how we help. And so it is.

Chapter Three

Raising Your Frequency

This is a vibrational frequency world.

Quantum physicists have taught for decades that everything is energy. This is not a matter-based world—it is an energy-based reality. At the core of the chair you're sitting on, the floor beneath your feet, and the desk in front of you is not solid matter, but invisible energy vibrating at a particular frequency—energy that takes form only when observed or touched.

To the logical human mind, this is a foreign concept. Even though quantum physics has proven this repeatedly, most people still believe that if they can see it, touch it, or feel it, it must be real.

And yet, the opposite is true: what we perceive as real is simply vibrating energy taking form in our awareness.

This changes everything about how we experience life on Earth. Once we understand that everything—including our physical body—is vibrating energy, we begin to see how powerful we truly are.

Our bodies are temporary costumes powered by a sacred vibrational force.

This is why many modern healers emphasize raising our vibrational frequency as a path to wellness. Practices like sound healing, acupuncture, and physical movement shift the body's energy into a higher state. I've always known that, for me, movement is one of the most basic and powerful energy shifters.

In my early thirties, when I was steeped in grief from losing loved ones, I worked at a fitness club. That studio vibrated with high energy—people exercising, laughing, sharing goals. Just walking into the space lifted me, no matter how deep my grief.

Today, we understand that opening our hearts and sending love out to the world creates an extraordinarily high frequency—not only in our bodies, but in everyone we touch.

Think of this universe as a vibrational soup, where every thought, emotion, and intention ripples out, affecting others. Emotions like love, joy, humor, and gratitude vibrate so rapidly and brightly that they naturally elevate the energy around them.

You are powerful!

You can walk into a coffee shop, take a deep breath, and silently send unconditional love to every person there—and the room will shift.

Of course, we've all experienced the opposite—walking into a room filled with tension or sadness. The energy feels heavy, and we instinctively contract. But remember, you are a golden being of divine light. You have the power to shift any vibration you encounter, whether in a workplace, a relationship, or the world itself.

Your divine love transforms everyone and everything – including yourself.

Even in dark energy spaces—like the haunted houses of New Orleans where I grew up—fear will only feed the darkness. But love, especially when channeled from the God-source through your heart chakra, will dispel fear instantly.

Love is the antidote to fear. Light is the antidote to darkness.

Nothing can harm you when you are radiating unconditional love.

Nature is another powerful energy shifter. Whether you walk in your neighborhood, hike in the mountains, or sit in your backyard with the birds and butterflies—nature will raise your frequency and bring healing. You don't need to fixate on your problems—just step outside and let Mother Earth do her work.

Music, too, is a divine frequency tool. A favorite song, a healing melody, or even subtle frequency apps playing in the background can lift your spirit. You can even play these tones while you sleep.

Animals are another divine gift. They are pure sentient beings of light who help us feel unconditional love. Go love on your dog, your cat, your horse—or sit with the butterflies and birds. These are sacred interactions with the divine and they open our hearts.

Even inanimate objects hold energy. Yes, even your car! When treated with love and gratitude, things tend to function better. The universe is alive. Everything vibrates.

You are not a passive participant here—you are a powerful transformer of energy.

The angels remind us that we can always connect to the God-source of unconditional love.

Try this: Close your eyes and say, "Angels, help me feel the flow of divine love." Visualize golden light flowing into you, through your crown chakra, and radiating out from your heart into the world. Picture your heart as a glowing golden globe of love, sending out waves of high-frequency healing energy.

This practice can reset your day, prepare you for challenges, or simply realign you to your divine purpose.

Let Go of Control: Feel Your Energy Shift Up to a Higher Frequency

Trusting in angelic guidance means letting go of the need to control every aspect of your life. When you surrender control, you allow the angels to guide you in ways that are often unexpected - but always for your highest good.

This means releasing attachment to specific outcomes and being open to a path that feels different from what you had planned.

The human mind tells us we are in control of everything that happens on earth. The higher soul knows this isn't true. The higher soul understands the importance of surrendering to the flow of unconditional love that aligns us with the highest good for all.

This divine surrender lightens our energy significantly and opens us to the new and better.

Chapter Three Summary: Raising Your Frequency – The Vibration of Love and Gratitude

- This is an energetic, vibrational universe—not a matter-based reality—as proven by quantum physics.

- Everything is energy, including your physical body, which is simply a vibrating costume for your soul.

- Healing and well-being come from raising your vibrational frequency through practices like sound healing, acupuncture, movement, and intentional thought.

- Movement and physical activity are powerful energy shifters; even environments filled with movement (like gyms) raise your energy.
- Emotions such as love, joy, gratitude, and humor vibrate at high frequencies and have the power to transform any space or interaction.
- You are a divine energetic being who can shift the frequency of any room simply by radiating love.
- Fear feeds dark energy, but unconditional love transforms and dissolves it.
- Nature, music, frequency tones, and interactions with animals are all natural tools to raise your vibration.
- Even inanimate objects hold vibrational energy—your thoughts and feelings influence how well material things function.
- The heart chakra is your gateway to divine love—visualizing it as a golden globe helps anchor and radiate love into the world.
- Angels speak the language of love. They are always near, helping you raise your frequency to connect with them and your departed loved ones.
- A channeled angelic message reminds us that love is our superpower, the highest gift of the human experience, and

the reason we incarnated on Earth.

A Channeled Message from The Angels

Beloved One,

We are with you every day. We are reaching out, lifting your energy so you can feel us with you and align with the divine.

We dwell in the frequency of love. If you cannot feel us, open your heart with a little gratitude, laughter, or kindness. These are the frequencies that lift you into our realm.

When you're feeling overwhelmed, picture us. See an angel in your mind's eye. Ask the Angel to show you light, to wrap you in wisdom. We can lift you out of your earthly story and into the realm of love and healing.

This is who we are. This is how we help.

Your greatest superpower is love. It's infinitely more important than your thoughts; more enlightening than your mind.

Feel our unconditional love.

Go out into the world and quietly send unconditional love to everyone you interact with today. This puts you in the flow of your own superpower as a divine being, as an Angel on earth.

You came to Earth to feel this unconditional love, to share it, and transform the world through it. This is your purpose as part of our Angelic team. And so it is.

Chapter Four

Prayer as Power

It's important to understand how to pray from the highest source to the highest source—not from the ego.

When you're in pain, longing, or needing help, pause and ask yourself: Who is praying? Is it my fearful ego or my wise, loving soul?

When the ego prays, it asks for worldly success—victory, wealth, recognition. But when the soul prays, it asks to be uplifted; to be held in grace, inner strength and wisdom.

Our higher self only seeks to understand what the current challenge is trying to teach us.

The soul prays to fulfill its divine purpose. That prayer is always answered.

There's a difference between saying, "Please God, help me win my game today," and praying, "Divine Beloved, lift me to the highest frequency of love, empowerment, forgiveness, and success. Remove all obstacles in my path to fulfilling my soul's mission. And so it is."

When I was in the hospital with a colon cancer diagnosis, I did not pray to be healed. I didn't ask for the cancer to disappear. I've held too many beloveds in my arms as they transitioned. I understand now that healing prayers aren't always answered in the way we expect.

Instead, I prayed: "Divine Beloveds, Source and Angels, lift me above my fear and pain. Bring me into a higher understanding of the purpose of this challenge - so I can move through it with grace and courage and fulfill my soul's work. And so it is."

That prayer was completely answered.

I also prayed for discernment—to see the light in each choice I was facing and to follow that light in all of my earthly decisions.

When I met with various surgeons, I didn't decide which one to choose based on logic or credentials. Instead, I checked in with my heart, my intuition, my senses. If I felt a "no," I honored it—even if the surgeon had every accolade.

I moved forward with courage and trust. I chose with love, and that choice led me to light. Those prayers were answered.

Do we always get what we want when we pray? We get what our soul wants, not what our ego desires. Our soul is in charge of every moment of our lives.

This is why it's important to distinguish between praying from ego and praying from soul. A dogmatic church might teach that if we pray hard enough and live righteously, we'll get what we ask for. That is not how the universe works. That's ego-based thinking.

Our soul is here to evolve, love more deeply, lift into higher consciousness, and help others do the same. That's what it prays for. It's not asking for a new luxury car—it's asking for divine alignment.

If your soul came here to do great work and it's not time for you to leave this life, then when illness or challenge show up and you ask for the lesson and the courage to rise, miracles unfold.

But that's not what you were praying for—you were praying to be aligned with divine will. And that prayer always brings peaceful empowerment and right action.

Crossing into the heavenly realms—what we call death—is not a tragedy. It is a homecoming. It is not the end. It is the ecstatic rejoining of our higher self with the God Source.

So don't ever think that someone died because they didn't pray hard enough. The greatest miracle of all is that we get to leave this earthly realm and return to divine love.

Some of my favorite prayers growing up were from my Catholic tradition. The Lord's Prayer remains one of the highest-frequency prayers we can say.

"Our Father who art in Heaven, hallowed be Thy name..." —those words lift us into connection, understanding, and grace.

In Unity Ministry School, I studied the prayer's original Aramaic translation. In that form, it's deeply sacred and full of divine power. It emphasizes the intimate and creative relationship between humanity and the divine.

Here is a translation used in Unity Worldwide Ministries and on their website:

Our Father who art in Heaven:

This phrase is translated as "Abwoon d'bwashmaya," which means "O Birther! Father-Mother of the Cosmos, you create all that moves in light."

Hallowed be Thy name:

The vibrational energy of the name for God is sacred. It vibrates within us in the "sacred place of the most high." We "hallow" that name by allowing its vibration to define our very being—and by seeing ourselves as temples of God's energy.

Thy kingdom come:

In Aramaic, this phrase is "teytey malkuthakh." Teytey describes a bridal chamber, site of union and fertility. Malkuthakh comes from an ancient name for Divine Mother; it refers to a womb. The overall image in Aramaic is that we nurture and give birth to the kingdom of God within us.

Thy will be done on earth, as it is in heaven:

God perfectly expresses in that sacred womb within me. With this affirmation, I choose to let the inner possibility and the outer manifestation be the same. In Aramaic, the word translated as "will" more accurately means "heart's desire."

Give us this day our daily bread:

This is the first actual request in the prayer—here we shift our focus from God to self. It completes a sacred contract: I will birth your heaven within me and you will see to my needs. "Lachma" in Aramaic is both "bread" and "understanding."

And forgive us our debts, as we also have forgiven our debtors:

The Aramaic word for debt means "failures" or "mistakes. The tense is important: we must have forgiven others before we can claim our own forgiveness.

And leave us not in temptation, but deliver us from evil:

The Aramaic phrase is: "Don't let us remain in" temptation. The Aramaic word for temptation means: "unripeness."

For thine is the kingdom and the power and the glory forever:

The Aramaic might more accurately be translated as "Through you the kingdom, through you the energy of life, through you the harmony of all things"

Personally, I love the power and insight of that original interpretation; it lifts the frequency of our eternal conversations with God.

As a child, I was deeply drawn to the Divine Mother, known in Catholicism as the Virgin Mary. But the word "virgin" in Aramaic means "pure-hearted" or "good soul"—not a woman untouched by man. That mis-translation has caused confusion and repression of women for centuries.

As a child growing up Catholic, this was my daily prayer:

"Remember, O most gracious Virgin Mary, that never was it known that anyone who fled to your protection, implored your help or sought your intercession, was ever left unaided. Inspired by this confidence, I fly unto thee, O Virgin of virgins, my Mother. To thee I come, before thee I stand. Humble and aware. Mother of the word incarnate, in thy mercy hear and answer me. Amen"

I prayed this millions of times in my childhood. I always received divine comfort.

Today, my home is filled with statues of Mary, the angels, Buddha and several Hindu deities such as Ganesha, the remover of obstacles. I know in my heart that every great spiritual tradition carries a pathway to God—not the punishing parts of the dogma, but the uplifting, heart-opening practices and beliefs.

In Unity Church, where I was ordained, we begin our prayers affirmatively:

"I affirm that I am a divine being who came to Earth on purpose with a powerful soul mission. I am fulfilling that mission now. Nothing will stop me. And so it is."

That kind of prayer aligns you with divine grace and power.

And yes, the angels hear our prayers. More than that—they pray beside us.

You've never uttered a word to God or cried out in pain without angels being right there beside you. They catch your words, lift your energy, and guide you into sacred light.

Even if your prayer sounds desperate or clumsy, the angels know what you mean. They lift you through time and space into the heavenly realms where you feel healed, whole, and loved. When you return to your earthly life, you carry divine strength.

All that matters is lifting your gaze from this physical world to the higher realms; acknowledging the higher consciousness of our divine universe.

And in that remembering of your true nature as part of a loving God Consciousness – you remember your own powerful holy essence.

This is the true meaning and power of prayer.

Your prayers are always heard. And always answered – for the highest good of all. And so it is.

Guided Meditation: Angelic Support for Life Challenges

Step One: Close your eyes. Take 3 deep breaths. Feel a warm golden light moving down from the crown chakra filling your vision and all of your senses with light.

Step Two: Focus your attention upwards and ask for guidance from the angelic realm. Say: Divine angelic beings lift me up in this moment. Open my heart. Quiet my mind.

Step Three: Picture beings of light standing around you with their arms open in loving support. Feel their unconditional love surrounding you until it makes you smile.

Step Four: Standing within the circle of Angelic light say: "I'm having trouble with this problem in my life." Name the problem. Take a breath and ask: "Can you resolve or heal this problem? I surrender it to you. Take it from me and lift it into the heavenly realms where all problems are solved and all answers are found."

Step Five: Allow yourself to trust that this is a divine loving universe and you are part of the perpetual love and grace that comes from the God Source. You are part of God. God is part of you. This opens your heart and quiets your mind. Let it all go. Stay in this trusting silence for three minutes.

Step Six: Ask, "What is mine to do with this problem? What are the steps I need to take to resolve this for highest good?" Sit in the stillness for one more moment listening.

Step Seven: Pick up a pen and paper and begin writing whatever words come through your pen to the paper. Allow them to flow without questioning or editing. You're taking notes from the divine. You're a secretary for the divine. Trust the process.

Step Eight: Ask, "Is there anything else I need to know?" Open your mind. Release your attachments to how you think this problem should be solved and receive whatever thoughts, images, words or feelings come to you. Write them quickly. Prompts to aid the process: I am feeling... I am hearing... I am knowing...

Step Nine: Trust that this problem is being worked on by the angelic realms. Surrender it to them. They are lifting you above the human mind. From now on, when you think of this problem know that it is already being solved. Let it go. Do not take any action or say any words about this problem for several hours. When you come back to this, you will have new insights and clarity of action.

Chapter Four Summary: Prayer as Power – Asking to Be Lifted

- Praying from Soul vs. Ego: True prayer comes from the soul, not the ego. The ego asks for outcomes; the soul asks for upliftment, understanding, and alignment with divine will.

- Soul-Based Prayer Is Always Answered: When we pray to be

guided, strengthened, and aligned with our soul's purpose, that prayer is answered every time.

- During my colon cancer experience, I didn't pray to be healed. I prayed for courage, understanding, and to receive the lesson with love. That prayer was fully answered.

- Discernment as Part of Prayer: Always use intuitive guidance to discern between choices—like choosing a surgeon. If the idea of making that choice lifts you into a frequency of happiness, love and sacred knowingness – it's the right choice for you.

- We Receive What the Soul Wants, Not the Ego: Prayers aligned with the soul's evolution bring miracles—not always the ones we imagined, but the ones we most need.

- Crossing Over Is Not a Failure: Death is not a tragedy or failure of prayer. It is a return to the divine realms. The greatest miracle is our soul's journey home.

- Powerful Prayers from Childhood: The Lord's Prayer and the Memorare to the Divine Mother were foundational healing tools in my early life and remain powerful today.

- Reclaiming Divine Mother Wisdom: Reframe the title, Virgin Mary, to pure-hearted Divine Mother. This honors her as a source of compassion and healing.

- Sacred Symbols and Inclusivity: Statues of Mary, angels, and Buddha fill my home as sacred reminders of the many faces of God; honoring the divine pathways in all traditions lifts our hearts.

- Unity's Affirmative Prayer: "I affirm that I am a divine being with a powerful soul mission..." is a model of high-frequency, soul-aligned prayer.

- Angels Pray Beside Us: The angels are always present during prayer, lifting our words and helping us rise—no matter how we pray or what we say.

- Healing Through Divine Frequency: When we pray, we are transported into higher realms, where healing, strength, and love are received before we return to face our earthly challenges with courage and grace.

A Channeled Message from The Angels

Beloved One,

Today we're sharing a powerful Angel prayer. You can use this whenever you need help:

Angels! I feel your love. I trust you. Show me a way through the darkness. Hold me in the light until my vision only sees light. Hand me the sword of unconditional love for today and every day. This Angel sword slices through darkness, fear, hatred and doubt. It causes no harm. Yet it transforms everything. All of my fears worries and wounds become shining gifts of beauty and light. Angels, wrap me in the cloak of heavenly beauty and sacred brilliance. And so it is.

Chapter Five

Listening to Light

How do angels speak to us?

They come to us through dreams, subtle signs, sacred numbers, audible messages, visual cues, and synchronistic events. These divine messengers use every frequency available to reach us—because they are our first responders on Earth, our most accessible and devoted helpers.

One of the most common angelic signals is numerical guidance. As a lifelong master numerologist and author of ***The Sacred Numerology Workbook***, I've been teaching clients for decades exactly how numbers serve as messages from the angelic realm. I love the sacred numbers—double digits like 11, 22, 33, 44—and the repeating triple numbers that catch our eye and make us pause. These are nudges from our angels, reminders to raise our frequency, to pay attention, and to awaken to our own Angelic presence.

I often hear clients say, "My favorite number has always been three." And when I reveal that their soul mission birth path is a 3, based on their numerology chart, they light up with realization. The angels have been speaking to them their whole life—through numbers!

Another powerful way angels connect is through auditory guidance. Their voices come through in moments of stillness, often when we're not thinking about anything in particular. Their tone is always kind, high-frequency, and uplifting—different from the voices of departed loved ones, spirit guides, or the God Source. Their voices carry the purity of celestial choirs—like sacred music from childhood.

Synchronicities are powerful signs: Someone with a familiar name appears just when you were thinking of that person; a book falls off a shelf with the exact wisdom you needed; you hear the same message repeated three times in a day from unrelated sources. These moments are not random—they are the angels aligning circumstances to deliver guidance.

One of my deepest practices for receiving guidance is channeled writing. I begin with quiet meditation, then ask the angels a specific open-ended question. I write fast, with no editing, allowing their wisdom to flow through me. Over the years, I've realized I've always been channeling their voices when I write—since childhood.

As a journalist in the 1980s, I wrote from the logical mind as a reporter in a newsroom. But later, I embraced my ability to allow the words to flow with inspiration. Now I recognize the frequency difference: Angelic guided writing is fluid, effortless, and brimming with love. Their messages pour in like notes from heaven. The key is to write quickly—no judgment, no editing. Just receive.

Of course, discernment is essential.

How do we know if a message is truly from the angels?

Messages from the human mind come with worry, fear, obligation, or a sense of heaviness. They feel like "ugh" in your body. But angelic messages feel light, loving, safe, and empowering. They uplift you and fill you with clarity.

I remember a moment when my daughter's school called and told me to take her to the hospital for a possible concussion. I was terrified. But as I drove to the school, the angels came to me and said: "Don't worry. Here's what will happen." They described the day's upcoming events—and every word came true. Their loving message dissolved my panic and filled me with trust.

Another profound moment came during my cancer diagnosis. I had many choices to make and constantly asked the angels for guidance. They showed me which option carried the light—and that was the path I followed. It didn't remove the pain, but it made the journey smoother, more courageous, and more connected to divine flow.

That's the power of listening to the light. When logic tells you to choose one path, but the angels shine their loving light on another, always choose the light. It will guide you through your darkest hour.

How to Practice Daily Channeled Writing with Angels

- Begin with meditation. Use the Om Shivaya mantra described in Chapter One.

- Pull out your pen and paper. Ask the angels an open-ended question like: - "Tell me more about how to solve this problem." - "Guide me toward the best direction for this project." - "Help me cope better with my mother's illness."

- Start writing—fast. Even if you haven't heard the answer yet, write the question repeatedly. Soon, you'll feel the flow.

- Let the words pour through. You'll feel like you're taking dictation from heaven. Their answers will come fast and full of love.

- Don't edit. Don't analyze. Just keep writing until it slows naturally.

- Then read. Go back and gently review their wisdom. You may clean it up a bit, but the core of it is your sacred message.

The Power of Asking

Angels are always available to offer guidance, but because they respect our free will, they wait for us to ask for their help. When we consciously reach out to them, they respond with loving, gentle support, helping to steer us in the right direction. Whether you are seeking guidance for a career change, relationship decision, or spiritual growth, the angels provide insights that align with your soul's purpose.

It's important to note that angelic guidance often comes as a quiet, inner knowing—a nudge from your intuition. The angels communicate in subtle ways, encouraging you to trust yourself and the divine plan for your life. By learning to listen to their gentle whispers and recognize their signs, you can access their wisdom more easily.

Calling on Specific Angels for Guidance

I've always seen Angels as beings of divine light without an earthly form such as a body or a gender. But for people raised in religious environments, Angels will often take the appearance of Biblical Archangels as a way to offer guidance in a familiar way.

Here are some of the key Archangel types to call upon if this is your preferred way to communicate with Angels:

Archangel Michael: Guidance for Protection and Courage

Archangel Michael is known as the angel of protection and strength. If you're feeling vulnerable, anxious, or afraid, Archangel Michael can offer you courage to move forward with confidence. He helps clear away fear and negativity, allowing you to make empowered decisions from a place of strength.

Prayer to Archangel Michael: I call upon you for protection and guidance. Please shield me from fear and doubt, and help me find the courage to move forward with confidence. I trust in your strength and wisdom.

Archangel Raphael: Guidance for Healing and Health

As the angel of healing, Archangel Raphael provides guidance for those seeking physical, emotional, or spiritual healing. If you're dealing with health challenges or emotional wounds, Raphael offers comfort and shows you the steps toward healing. His guidance often comes through intuitive nudges that help you make decisions for your highest well-being.

Prayer to Archangel Raphael: I call upon you for healing and guidance. Please support me on my healing journey and lift me into a higher frequency of health and well-being.

Archangel Gabriel: Guidance for Communication and Clarity

Archangel Gabriel is known as the angel of clarity of expression. If you're struggling to find your voice or need help expressing yourself,

Gabriel can help you. This angel also helps with gaining clarity on life's big decisions and finding confidence to move forward in your soul's purpose.

Prayer to Archangel Gabriel: I call upon you for clarity and guidance. Please help me communicate my truth with power and grace. Help me speak from my deepest soul's wisdom. Show me the path forward with clarity.

Archangel Uriel: Guidance for Wisdom and Insight

Archangel Uriel is the angel of wisdom and light. If you're seeking deeper understanding or divine insights about a particular situation, Uriel can help illuminate the way. His guidance often comes through flashes of inspiration, sudden realizations, or moments of joyful inner knowing.

Prayer to Archangel Uriel: I call upon you for insight. Illuminate my path and help me see truth with clarity and understanding. I quiet my mind and trust in your divine light to guide me forward.

Recognizing The Signs

Once you've called on the angels, it's important to stay open to the signs they send in response. These signs may come in different forms, and it's up to you to remain aware and receptive. Here are some common ways angels communicate their guidance:

-**Repeating Numbers:** If you frequently see the same numbers—such as 111, 222, or 444—this is often a sign from the angels. Each number carries its own message (See my Sacred Numerology reference in Chapter 8) and angels use these numbers to catch your attention. For example, seeing 444 may indicate that the angels are surrounding you with divine strength.

-**Birds and Butterflies:** If you find yourself seeing the same bird repeatedly and the bird seems to be speaking to you – listen. Birds and butterflies are spirit messengers from the highest realms. If you're surrounded by butterflies, trust that the Angels and your departed loved ones are giving you kisses and hugs. Speak to them out loud and listen for their responses.

-**Dreams:** Angelic messages often come through dreams and dream visions. If you have a vivid dream where you feel the presence of an angel or a departed loved one you are receiving their sacred help, guidance and healing. Trust that this is divine guidance. Keep a notepad by your bedside to record your dream visions.

-**Music:** Angelic messages are often delivered through music because music is a powerful frequency shifter. You may hear a song that resonates with your situation or contains lyrics that speak directly to you. Pay attention to how certain songs make you feel and trust the messages the higher beings are sending you through music.

-**Intuition:** The most direct form of angelic guidance is intuition. If you suddenly feel a strong sense of knowing what you need to do; or you get a gut feeling about a decision or relationship - trust it. The angels guide us through intuition, helping us make choices that align with our highest good. If you feel it in your gut in an empowering way – not a fearful way – it's from the Angelic Realms.

Trusting the Guidance You Receive

Angelic guidance is always loving, supportive, and aligned with your highest good, but it may not always be the answer you expect or want. The key is to surrender how your human self wants things to go, be open to divine guidance and willing to follow the path that unfolds before you.

If you're unsure about the guidance you've received, don't hesitate to ask the angels for confirmation. They will provide additional nudges to reassure you. Trust that the angels have your best interests at heart and that their guidance will always lead you toward wisdom, growth, and spiritual empowerment.

Chapter Five Summary – Listening to Light: Receiving Divine Guidance

- Angels communicate in many ways: dreams, signs, sacred numbers, voices, visuals, and synchronicities.
- Angels are always available to offer guidance, but because they respect our free will, they wait for us to ask for their help.
- Angels will often take the appearance of Biblical Archangels as a way to offer guidance in a familiar way; trust that however they appear to you is perfectly designed for your highest good and comfort.
- Once you've called on the angels, it's important to stay open to the signs they send in response which can include numbers, dreams and music.
- Sacred numerology is a clear and accessible method for receiving angelic messages.
- Double and triple repeating numbers are divine nudges to awaken, learn, or shift your frequency.

- Auditory messages from angels have a distinct, high-frequency sweetness—unlike any other voice.
- Synchronicities (divine timing and alignments) are one of their favorite tools.
- Channeled writing is a powerful practice to receive detailed guidance.
- Discernment is key: ego messages feel heavy and fearful; angelic messages feel light and loving.
- Trust the path with the light—it is divinely guided even through struggle.
- Everyone can access these messages. The angels are always speaking—we just need to listen.

A Channeled Message from The Angels

Beloved One,

Whenever you call out to us we hold you in the highest light where nothing and no one can hurt you. Surrender to this inner knowing that you are protected. We stand beside you in light.

We lift you above fear. Fear is not your friend even though we know it is a popular earth emotion. We urge you to give your fear to us. We transform it into love and wisdom so that you feel empowered and open hearted.

Feel us right now taking one of your darkest fears away, lifting it into the light. Now it shatters into a million shards of golden divine energy - illuminating all around you. You will feel that fear no more. And so it is.

Chapter Six

Forgiveness

When we think of ascendancy, it means remembering that we are beings of light rising up to our highest frequency of consciousness. That frequency is unconditional love, compassion, empowerment, and alignment with the God-Source energy.

The opposite of that high frequency is the heavy energy of blame, anger, and judgment—those are the burdens we carry in our hearts when we're unable to forgive. And yes, it's true: Earth is a realm where we experience deep pain and betrayal. There are humans who hurt others, who break hearts irresponsibly, and who act without awareness. You have likely known someone who didn't love you the way they should have, who misled you, or even caused you great suffering.

Your human mind may want to label them as bad, to judge or condemn them, to hold on to that pain and never forgive. But in this book—and in all true spiritual teachings—we are being asked to rise into a higher awareness, to embody ascension, and to anchor in the frequency of love. You can't live in the higher frequencies while still dragging around the heavy stone of unforgiveness.

Forgiveness is for you. It's not about the other person. It's not condoning their behavior. It's about releasing the poison of resentment and vindictiveness from your own system. It's about lightening your emotional load so you can ascend as the Angelic being you came to be. It's not your job to judge another person's soul journey. When we leave the body, our soul is held gently by our angels, guides, and the God-source to lovingly review our lifetime; we see and feel the ripple effect of all of our choices, words, and actions. We deeply feel how we affected others. But we feel it from a place of higher awareness. Not punishment—but as an awakening. We say, "Ah, I see now. I should have loved more. I could have chosen courage. I could have lifted out of fear." That soul review becomes the catalyst for our evolution.

Even the murderer is not yours to judge. They will face their own soul's awakening, far more illuminating than anything you could ever say or do. So the real question becomes: Why would I choose to carry this heavy energy of judgment, blame, or anger when it only hurts me?

When you realize you're not responsible for anyone else's soul, only your own, and that your only job is to grow your light—then the need for judgment falls away. Forgiveness becomes the master key to your ascension.

While writing this book, the angels have shown up at divine moments to hand me synchronicities; to show me I was on track and provide experiences needed for the book. And today, just as I was preparing to write about forgiveness, an old friend—someone I've had distance from—called me out of the blue. We had once been very close, but judgments had quietly pushed us apart. We hadn't resolved anything—just drifted. And today, we didn't rehash the past. We didn't even name the thing that created the rift. Instead, we simply loved each other. We asked about each other's lives. We supported each other. And it felt beautiful. Light. Free. Aligned with the God-source.

That's the miracle of forgiveness. It lifts your frequency. It clears the blocks between souls. And it opens the heart to love again.

But I realize that forgiveness can be especially hard when someone has caused deep, irreversible loss—especially the loss of a child. I've worked with many parents whose children died at the hands of drunk drivers or from fentanyl-laced drugs unknowingly received from friends.

As a human, I hold these parents in deepest compassion. Their grief is sacred. Their anger is understandable. But over time, through prayer and meditation, many of these parents have reached into their highest knowing and received divine messages from their children in spirit:

> "We made a soul agreement. I loved you always and still do. I'm right beside you. The friend who played the role of my destroyer was a part of our soul plan too. We all agreed to raise the frequency of those who love us, through this very pain. To teach compassion, forgiveness, and gratitude—because these are the highest vibrations humans can carry on Earth."

This is not easy to grasp. It takes spiritual maturity and courage. It demands we see life through our soul's lens—not the human lens of blame and punishment. But I've witnessed these transformations. I've watched grieving parents shift their frequency, meditate on the soul agreement, and even send love to the person who caused the tragedy. That love, which comes from the God-source, is transformational for all involved – the forgiver and the forgiven.

In my Soul Agreements classes, we use sacred numerology to understand the karmic contracts we've made with those who have hurt us. It's one of the most healing tools available to humans. When you realize that the person who caused you pain is part of your soul plan for growth—it lifts the veil of misunderstanding. It doesn't excuse harmful actions. But it places them in the context of soul evolution.

Maybe that soul loved you enough to play the "bad actor" in this lifetime for your growth—and theirs.

I ask only that you consider this. Meditate on it. And when you're ready, here's a simple, powerful forgiveness practice:

A Forgiveness Practice

Close your eyes.- Picture the person you've been unable to forgive.-

See them as a soul—not as a human personality, but as a fellow soul on a journey, doing the best they can at their level of awareness.-

Now, channel golden, unconditional love from the God-source into your heart.

Breathe it in. Let it fill your chest.

Then send that love from your heart Chakra to their soul. No words. Just energy. Just love.

Now imagine them looking back at you with a smile—full of love, gratitude, understanding.

Hold that vision. Then release.

Do this once or twice a day, just 30 seconds. You'll begin to see that person differently. You'll feel lighter. More loving. More empowered.

The energy between you will begin to heal without any words being spoken.

In truth, forgiveness sets you free. And from that place of freedom, you can rise into your ascended mastery. You can live your soul's greatest mission.

You can Angel Up.

Chapter Six Summary: Forgiveness — The Master Ascension Key

- Ascendancy means rising into the frequency of unconditional love, compassion, and God-source energy.
- Unforgiveness anchors us in lower energies such as blame, anger, and judgment—preventing spiritual ascension.
- Forgiveness is not about condoning behavior; it's about releasing yourself from emotional burdens that block your light.
- We are not here to judge others' soul journeys—each soul will review its own life after death with love and awareness.
- Forgiveness is a gift to yourself, allowing you to live your highest potential and fulfill your soul mission.
- Divine timing brought a personal forgiveness opportunity to me just before writing this chapter—a reminder that healing is always supported by the angels.
- True forgiveness can happen without words, simply by sharing love and presence in a soul-to-soul connection.
- Even in cases of profound loss, such as a child's death, forgiveness can be found through understanding soul agreements made in the higher realms.
- The soul agreement teaching, combined with sacred numerology, helps explain why difficult people enter our lives

for spiritual growth.

- Soul contracts are made out of love, even when the role played in this lifetime appears tragic or harmful.

- Forgiveness practice: - See the person as a soul. - Channel golden, unconditional love from the God-source. - Send it to their soul through your heart chakra. - See them smile at you with gratitude and love. - Hold the vision. Then release.

- This practice lifts your frequency, heals emotional wounds, and helps you align with your divine mission.

- Forgiveness is the master key to ascension and a necessary step on the path to becoming the light you came here to be.

A Channeled Message from the Angels

Beloved one,

If you could see your earthly life from our perspective you would instantly understand that holding anger, blame, hatred towards anyone - only darkens your light. It weighs you down into the dense realms of humanity. It clouds your truth.

We never want that for you. We love you unconditionally and eternally. You are one of us as an Angel on earth.

Let us take that burden of unforgiveness from you right now. Feel the sacred release.

We are lifting you into the light of the highest realm of God Consciousness - where all pain is transformed instantly into divine love.

From this moment on, you will not remember what you were so blameful about; the story will shift in your memory. You'll see the light within every sacred moment of your story. And so it is.

Chapter Seven

The Seven Stones to Ascension

When we arrive on Earth, we are still connected to the heavenly realms—as babies, as children—and we are imbued with our soul's wisdom, understanding that we're here to wake up our consciousness and live from our higher self, even while walking on Earth.

And then life goes on. We get programmed, taught, trained, wounded, and suddenly we forget our higher self. We forget that we are part of a divine order beyond the physical. Then we hit a soul reinvention point. We experience one of the seven stones of human suffering.

These are the 7 Stones to Ascension on Earth:

1. Grief

2. Lack of Purpose

3. Disappointment in Others (the world at large)

4. Disappointment in Self (self-doubt)

5. Relationship Struggles

6. Health & Body

7. Spiritual Crisis

Stone One: Grief

When we lose someone we love, it is the great shattering of our world as we know it—and it is also our greatest moment of spiritual awakening on Earth. It is an opportunity to see beyond the veil and wake up to our divine essence.

I lost my beautiful young husband when I was 29. I've worked with so many people who, in their 20s, experienced devastating grief. Others, later in life, have lost a child or a partner.All of these moments of devastating loss feel like the shattering of life as we know it, but they wake us up to our higher self.

Grief is the great spiritual awakener. I've often called grief the greatest spiritual teacher on Earth because she breaks us wide open and shatters our understanding of the world.

And if we believe in a fundamentalist God that controls our lives and deaths, we may ask: Why did this happen to my loved one? If there is a loving God, how could this happen?

These questions push us to seek deeper meaning and truth. Certainly, when my husband died of colon cancer, I questioned everything. We thought we were invincible—and then I held him as he crossed over.

But all of the questions that grief stirs up are on purpose. They teach us that there is no death, that the veil is thin, and that we are eternal souls doing a soul review—not being judged by a punishing God.

> In Matthew 28:2, we read of the angel rolling away the stone from Jesus' tomb. The angel appears in radiant light and tells the grieving women not to be

> afraid—Jesus has ascended. This is a profound symbol of what grief teaches us: There is no death.

Every client I've worked with has been reshaped by grief. It destroys our old self so we can rebuild in alignment with the God source. Most importantly, we come to know the angels are helping us.

In the dark night of grief, the angels comfort us, lift our energy, and give us divine signs and miracles to keep going. Your beloved is with you. The angels surround you in love and healing.

They whisper to you: You are an accelerated soul. You signed up for big spiritual growth so you can become one of the great healers on Earth.

The gift of grief is learning what real love is—unconditional and eternal. You're shedding what no longer matters and aligning with your true mission. You are now an Ascended Master.

Prayer to the Angels to Lift Grief from Your Heart

Beautiful Angels, Lift this heavy weight from my heart. Take this stone of grief and shatter it into golden beams of love that spread around the world - helping others. Take this pain and transform it into light. This golden light lifts me into my higher soul where I see my beloved happy and healthy beside me. Let me hear their laughter. And so it is.

Affirmation For Overcoming Grief

I affirm that I am a powerful being of golden light – brighter than any darkness, more powerful than grief; my heart overflows with love and joy.

Summary of Stone One – Grief:

The Human Struggle:

The great shattering of losing a loved one destroys our old view of life, love, God, and our higher purpose.

The Angelic Reframe:

You're an accelerated soul who agreed to grow and evolve rapidly so you could become a powerful spiritual healer and teacher. The angels are with you through every heartbeat of grief.

The Gift on the Other Side:

You now embrace unconditional love, bring it to every relationship, and step into your true soul mission on Earth – fully aware of your departed beside you every step of the way.

Stone Two: Lack of Purpose

In everyone's life, there comes a moment when we lose our direction—when our sense of purpose slips away. Maybe you chose a career early on, only to realize it makes you miserable. Maybe you were laid off or your company closed. Maybe you've never worked before and suddenly find yourself thrust into the workforce, uncertain of who you are or what you're here to do.

These moments of uncertainty are not failures. They are sacred awakenings. Because every soul comes to Earth with a divine mission—a purpose unique to them. You arrived with innate talents, extraordinary gifts, and intuitive wisdom to help guide you on that path.

But your human mind often argues with your soul. It tells you a career in your passion isn't logical. That following your dream won't pay the bills. That's the great delusion—your mind talking you out of who you truly are and why you came.

Many people choose careers for financial security and later found themselves in despair. Financial security is not the goal and is rarely achievable. The only true security is remembering you are a divine being with a purpose and aligning your work with that purpose.

This is an energy-based universe. Everything you do vibrates a certain energy—your studies, your work, your dreams. And that energy shapes your world.

When you lose a job, it isn't failure. It's a soul nudge. A divine intervention. The angels are showing you that something toxic is ready to be released so you can ascend to your next chapter.

This is where Sacred Numerology becomes a beacon. I've taught and practiced it since 1980, guiding thousands of souls to rediscover their true work. Your numbers reveal your soul's mission and illuminate your reinvention points—but we'll explore this deeper in Chapter Eight.

For now, trust that your soul knows the way. And when your intuition nudges you toward something—even if it terrifies you—that's your inner guidance. That's your angelic support.

Take one step forward. Enroll in the class. Reach out to someone doing the work you're drawn to. Write your business plan. These are all ways of saying, "Yes, I'm ready."

The angels can't push you. But the moment you say yes, they'll surround you with synchronicities, divine surprises, and open doors.

When I work with clients, we always review their reinvention points—those moments when a career ended or a job was lost. Every single time, it eventually brought them to greater happiness, deeper alignment, and soulful abundance.

If you're reading this, you are not here to get a job, any job. You are here to do meaningful, high-frequency work that uplifts others and serves the world.

Your grief, your heartbreak, your longing—they're signs that you're an accelerated soul, ready to rise.

Let's release the false belief that says your spiritual gifts must be your weekend hobby or something you give away for free. The angels want you to create abundance from your soul's gifts. Maybe you're here to be a coach, a healer, a sacred numerologist, or a minister. Those titles may sound unconventional—but they are perfect for me, and they helped me build a joyful, successful life. You have the same potential waiting for you.

All you need is the courage to say: I surrender. I'm open. I'm ready.

A Prayer to the Angels to Reveal Your Soul's Purpose

Beautiful Angels, you see my great soul mission and the gifts I brought with me; show them to me. Whisper in my ear whenever I doubt my way. Bring me miracles that show my divine path forward. Open every door that leads to my highest and best purpose. And so it is.

Affirmation for Finding Purpose

I affirm that I am a powerful divine being who came here on purpose with a unique soul mission – and nothing and no one can stop me from accomplishing what I came here to do.

Summary of Stone Two – Lack of Purpose:

The Human Struggle of Lack of Purpose:

You feel completely lost, full of self-doubt. You're angry and blaming others—especially if you've been laid off. You feel depressed and afraid.

The Angelic Reframe of Lack of Purpose:

You have a divine soul plan, and the angels are revealing it in every way they can. They whisper it in your dreams, your meditations, your writing. They say, "Just take one step. Show us you're ready. We'll open every door."

The Gift on the Other Side:

You find a new purpose, a more aligned career.- You discover your soul's true work and create abundance your way. You are seen, valued, and loved for the work you were always meant to do.

Stone Three: Disappointment in the World

Today, as I write this book, I feel the immense heaviness of the world. So much conflict. So much turmoil. We are living in a time of extraordinary upheaval, especially here in the United States. I'm not alone in this feeling—I hear it daily from my clients, students, and friends. People are grieving. They're disappointed in our leaders—regardless of political affiliation—and terrified of the future. The very fabric of life seems to be unraveling.

From the human view—the ego's perspective—it truly feels like the end of the world. Division is everywhere. Light feels distant. And yet... this is only the human lens. The soul sees a deeper truth.

When we quiet the mind and rise into the higher view—the soul's view—we remember that Earth is a stage of light and dark. Good players and bad players. Each playing a vital role in the collective evolution of humanity. We chose to incarnate into this time of transformation. We knew it would be chaotic. And we said yes.

Yes, to anchoring the light. Yes, to being healers. Yes, to being warriors of love.

So the next time you're overwhelmed—by a news story or a disagreement—pause. Breathe. And pray: "Angels, please wrap your loving vision around my heart. Help me rise above the fear and remember why I came here."

With angelic help, we feel the light again.

> In 2014, I received a vision during a high fever. The angels held me in space above Earth, and I watched as beams of light shot up from the planet—piercing the

> darkness. Filling the shadows. They said, "You must remember, the light always wins. Love always wins."

I've never forgotten that. It has sustained me through these times. And I offer it now to you.

We cannot heal the world from a place of fear. We must rise. We must love. We must hold our light high.

This is our soul assignment: To love one another soul to soul. To stop arguing ideas. To stop needing to be right.

The darkness is only surfacing because it's ready to be healed.

The "bad players" are participating in a higher mission—to bring the darkness into the light. This is a time of collective soul healing.

And the angels? They are pouring light into every dark corner, standing by our side, waiting for us to ask.

This is how we shift the planet.

Each thought we think sends out ripples—of darkness or light. Ask yourself: What thoughts am I sending into the world today?

Am I spreading fear or faith? Judgment or love?

Trust divine order. Trust the higher plan. Trust that love still runs this extraordinary universe.

This is our way forward.

A Prayer to the Angels to Lift You from Disappointment

Beautiful Angels – Lift me up to see the heavenly view of our human world. Show me the powerful light that spreads into every dark corner of earth - illuminating everything and everyone with love. Show me the goodness of my fellow humans, their courageous loving hearts and how hard they try to get it right. Help me see beyond the personality and deep into the perfect divine essence of every human of earth. Teach me to be like you beautiful Angels – beings of compassionate wisdom and unconditional love. And so it is.

Affirmation for Overcoming Disappointment in the World

I am using my angelic powers to rise above this chaos. I am a warrior of light. I pour divine love into the world, even where I see darkness.

Summary Of Stone Three: Disappointment in the World

The Human Struggle:

We are living in fear, conflict, and pain. Everyone feels isolated and disconnected. Political and personal disagreements are fracturing relationships.

The Angelic Reframe:

Angels show us that everything must come to the surface to be healed. This is a time of collective transformation. Even in chaos, light and love are prevailing. In numerology, this is a 9 universal year: a time of surrender and spiritual completion.

The Gift on the Other Side:

We are being called to surrender the ego's need to be right. We are learning to love and support one another soul to soul. We are remembering that we came here to help lift the world into the light.

Stone Four: Disappointment in Self (Self-Doubt)

There is not a human walking this Earth who doesn't struggle with self-doubt. It's universal. It doesn't matter how successful, beautiful, or seemingly happy a person appears on the outside—inside, all humans wrestle with the same quiet voice of unworthiness. Why? Because self-doubt comes from the human mind—from the ego lens. Your soul is never disappointed in you.

Your soul knows that at every moment, you are doing your absolute best—according to your current level of awareness, consciousness, and healing. You came here as a perfect divine being, and your soul sees you as such. You are greater than every challenge and every circumstance. No matter how things look to your human self, you are doing an awesome job.

At the end of your life, when you lift out of your body, the only one who evaluates your journey is your own loving, wise higher self.

From my own experiences in the higher realms, and from what my departed loved ones have told me, the soul review is one of the most loving, nurturing, and insightful experiences you'll ever have. It is not scary. It does not shame you. You are held by angels, gently lifted into the higher perspective of your soul's journey. You'll see that you were wearing the "Earth costume," walking the soul plan you courageously agreed to live out.

> Simply by choosing to incarnate on Earth, you have already proven how brave and magnificent your soul truly is.

Souls in the higher realms understand how difficult it is to be human. Earth is a dense realm filled with intense emotional energies—fear, grief, anxiety, and yes, self-doubt—that make us forget who we really are.

In the higher realms, only unconditional love, wisdom, and compassion exist. We come to Earth to walk through this heaviness and experience the full spectrum of emotions—from soaring love and joy to the deepest despair and self-loathing.

In your soul review, you'll see how every thought, every feeling, every action affected those around you—and yourself.

You will see that you tried—over and over again—to be better, to do better. You'll forgive yourself for the mistakes you believed were unforgivable.

You'll also see where you might have chosen more love... where you could have been braver. But even this is shown to you with the utmost love and compassion.

Your angels will remind you: You are a being of goodness. Of courage. Of love. You'll see how fear never truly served you, and yet—you kept going. And that's what matters.

The gift of the soul review is this:

You realize you have always done your best. You love your soul for trying. And trying again.

As humans, we forget. We forget that we are divine beings who created a soul plan filled with challenges and gifts. Our free will allows us to choose: to grow and open our hearts, or to remain stuck in blame, pain, and fear. But something always happens—a health crisis, heartbreak, the death of a loved one—that awakens us. Every one of us has this awakening moment.

And when awakening happens, we remember: No one is punishing us. No one has ever judged us—except our own human mind.

Your higher self sees the truth: You are a beautiful soul of unconditional love and divine light. Self-doubt is a lie told by the human mind. That's why we meditate—to quiet the ego voice and hear the soul instead. When you quiet the mind, you can finally hear the truth:

You are a powerful, divine being doing the very best you can.

A Prayer to the Angels to Lift You from Self-Doubt

Beautiful angels, lift me up to see the journey of my soul—the awakening moments, the courage, the mistakes. Let me see it all through the eyes of my higher self, so that I can witness the beauty of my own goodness and the incredible strength I've carried into this lifetime. Help me, angels, to love my human self while I am still here—so that it cannot stop me with self-doubt. Help me see myself the way you see me: with compassionate wisdom and unconditional love, so that I am empowered to fulfill my soul's mission on Earth.

Affirmation for Overcoming Self-Doubt

I am a powerful divine being who came here on purpose with a courageous soul mission. I am doing the best I can at every step of my evolution.

Summary of Stone Four: Disappointment in Self (Self-Doubt)

The Human Struggle:

We feel unworthy, incompetent, unlovable. The human mind says: Who do you think you are? You're not good enough to be loved, to succeed, to be happy.

The Angelic Reframe:

Each of us is a perfect divine being of light and love, born with a courageous heart and sacred soul mission. When we remember this truth, we are empowered to try again and find the gift in every challenge.

The Gift on the Other Side:

We learn that self-doubt is just a voice from the human mind. Through meditation and spiritual practice, we quiet that voice and hear the truth of the soul: You are powerful. You are light. You are love. And so it is.

Stone Five: Relationship Struggles

Every relationship in your life is a soul agreement made before this lifetime began—for the highest good of all involved. You agreed to experience both the most loving and the most painful relationships on purpose. You knew that they would push both of you to expand your consciousness, open your heart, and remember your soul missions for this lifetime.

(Sacred numerology helps you understand the purpose and pitfalls of each of these relationships, and we will explore that more in Chapter Eight.)

It's essential to remember that all relationships are serving your highest good, no matter how they play out. From my own out-of-body and shared death experiences—where I've been visited by my departed and shown how divine order works—what I know to be true is this:

> The ones who hurt us the most love us the most as souls in our heavenly soul posse.

In the soul realm, these are our greatest soul mates and most sacred soul agreements. They love us unconditionally. And at the end of our lifetime, when we take our final breath and rise into the heavenly dimensions, we are greeted by our soul posse—even those who hurt us while we were on Earth.

We are held by angels as we see the backstory of every person we believed did us wrong. We feel gratitude and unconditional love for them, realizing how they helped spark our soul's evolution.

Yes, we incarnated on Earth to bump into each other—for better or worse. That is the nature of our soul agreements.

The person you fall in love with, expecting a forever story, may break your heart—and yet that, too, is a beautiful soul agreement for your highest growth.

Partnerships aren't just about living happily ever after. They're here to help us evolve. And because the human ego drives most of our behavior, we inevitably hurt each other. That's the nature of the human condition.

Our souls, however, see these experiences as essential lessons. The higher self sees each relationship as part of the soul's sacred curriculum. There is no Hollywood love story—there is only evolution, compassion, and soul growth.

So how do you shift your perspective today and see every relationship—past and present—from this higher view? Whether it's the boss who fired you, the partner who betrayed you, or the person you blame for a devastating loss—

There's only one way: through meditation, quieting the ego mind, and lifting into your soul's wisdom.

Picture your beloved soul posse—all seated in a luminous circle on stone benches, radiant with golden light.

See every soul you've ever interacted with—those who loved you, those who hurt you.

See them smiling at you with unconditional love. And smile back. Say to them: Thank you so much for loving me, for helping me grow.

The angels help you see your relationships this way, here and now.

A Prayer to the Angels to Illuminate the Purpose of Your Relationships:

Beautiful angels, lift me up to see the heavenly circle of all the souls that I have made agreement with in this lifetime. Show me their great, beautiful hearts and their golden light. Help me remember that all humans—no matter how they behave—are divine beings in their essence. Our personalities may be flawed, but our souls are perfect and loving. Help me to see this, beautiful angels. Help me to love everyone on Earth as if I know who they really are. Help me, angels, to bring compassion and unconditional love to all relationships. And so it is.

Affirmation for Healing Relationships:

I affirm that I am a powerful divine being and that all humans who have affected me on Earth are part of my soul posse for highest good. I am grateful for every relationship—every person who has loved me, hurt me, or lifted me up. And so it is.

Summary of Stone Five: Relationship Struggles

The Human Struggle:

Relationships cause us great pain and sometimes wound us so deeply that we shut down our hearts and believe it's not safe to love. This isolates us and disconnects us from the world.

The Angelic Reframe:

Angels show us that every soul we've interacted with on Earth is part of our soul posse. The ones who hurt us the most love us the most and agreed to help us grow by playing the challenging roles.

The Gift on the Other Side:

There are no bad players in our lives. We are all divine beings who made soul agreements for the highest good of all. Recognizing this brings forgiveness, compassion, and wisdom.

Stone Six: Health and Body

Before we come to the human realm, each of us chooses our exact body, personality, and the health challenges and gifts we will experience in this lifetime. Our soul designs this so that the perfect lessons can be expressed through the body, especially when we need a powerful nudge to reinvent ourselves or remember who we truly are.

Our bodies are perfectly designed for the soul mission we have chosen. When we take our final breath and cross over, we realize that the body we struggled with held the perfect lessons. It shaped our growth and protected us from pitfalls. We see how elegantly it delivered our soul's curriculum.

This means that even when we take excellent care of our bodies—eating healthy foods, using supplements, exercising—we will still receive health nudges. It's part of life in the body. These nudges may come through genetic conditions, environmental exposures, or accidents.

> The deeper purpose of every health challenge is to wake us up and align us more fully with our soul path.

When our body is sick or injured, it demands our attention in a way that emotional pain often does not. We are called to reinvent our lives and awaken to a new understanding of ourselves.

Injuries also serve this purpose. A car accident, for example, may bring brain trauma that forces us to quiet the mind, live from the heart, and shift our entire way of being. Once we move through the pain, we may see the blessing it brought to our lives.

Our human bodies are vehicles of the soul's knowledge.

Last year, I was diagnosed with colon cancer. This diagnosis shook me. My first husband, Paul, died of colon cancer in 1980, and I had cared for him through that traumatic journey.

I had lived a healthy life ever since, consciously avoiding anything that might cause cancer. Yet suddenly, I was facing the very illness I had feared for decades. What an incredible wake-up call.

That diagnosis began a miraculous journey—guided by angels, supported by departed loved ones, and embraced by a circle of soul sisters offering healing and love.

My most important question became: What is the soul lesson in this illness? Not as a punishment, but as a sacred invitation. What is my soul asking me to shift so I can move through this with grace and light?

I received powerful inner guidance. I made changes in my work and my personal life. And with each moment of the health crisis, I asked myself, What is the soul gift in this moment?

I saw that our angels are already present during every painful, scary moment—offering healing and grace. But they can work even more powerfully when we say: 'Angels, help me. Heal me. Lift me above this.'

That prayer opens the channel. Their love pours in. Their healing light surrounds us.

So whatever you're struggling with today, know that there is a soul gift in it. When you walk the path with angels, you reduce your pain and suffering by lifting into love and understanding.

I also learned to open my heart to those around me—to pour unconditional love on everyone I interacted with when I was sick;

to ask about their lives, and see their goodness. This deepened my connection to the angels and the divine.

Some souls choose a path of physical suffering as an accelerated route for soul growth. We do not have to choose that path to evolve—but when we do, it can quickly burn through negativity and old patterns.

When Paul died of colon cancer, he had become a pure being of love and light. His illness stripped away all negativity and reconnected him completely to the God Source. It was an exalted state of consciousness. I was blessed to witness it.

Prayer to the Angels to Lift Us Above Our Suffering:

Beautiful angels, please lift me above this pain and suffering. Help me see it from the heavenly realms and remember what my body is trying to tell me. Help me embrace the gift in the experience. Remind me that my body is only a shell for my soul, and that my spirit can lift above the body at any moment. Teach me not to focus on the pain or the suffering, but to focus on the angels who are helping and healing me at every moment.

Affirmation for Healing the Body:

I affirm that I am a powerful and perfect divine being, and that perfect health is my birthright. I reclaim the memory that I am unstoppable golden light and unconditional love. All illness, injury, and tension of the body is released, and so it is.

Summary of Stone Six: Health and Body

The human struggle:

Each of us faces physical challenges—whether migraines, chronic illness, or injury. These struggles often pull us away from our higher wisdom and into fear or dependency on others' guidance, rather than listening to our own soul.

The angelic reframe:

Every illness and injury is a soul-designed nudge to help us remember who we are and realign with our divine mission. When we shift focus from the body to the angels around us, we receive deep healing and wisdom.

The gift on the other side:

We stop resisting the body and instead honor it for its sacred messages. We open our hearts, connect with our soul, and allow the angels to help us heal from a higher place.

Stone Seven: Spiritual Crisis

There's an epidemic of anxiety, depression, disconnection, and rage in our world today. Many of my clients describe panic attacks and crippling anxiety that lead them to medication. Often their children are on medication for anxiety. This reveals a deeper truth: we are in the midst of a collective spiritual crisis.

A collective spiritual crisis arises when we forget that we are divine beings—greater than any challenge or circumstance.

We are souls temporarily walking in human bodies. Our essence is light and love, and our true home is in the invisible, higher realms where our higher soul still resides.

When we remember that this entire universe is run by the God Source—unconditional love and divine order—we awaken. This sacred force pulses through every molecule of the universe. It flows through us all, no matter what we feel, believe, or how we behave.

What blocks us from this divine awareness? The human mind—an essential tool for navigating Earth—can also become our greatest obstacle. Its job is to keep us safe, which means it often leads with fear, anxiety, and overthinking. When we let it control our psyche, anxiety becomes our constant companion.

But when we quiet the mind—especially through meditative tools like chanting 'Om Namah Shivaya'—we return to our soul. We feel the presence of the God Source within us. We remember we are never separate from divine love and light.

The human mind puts blinders on us, blocking the light and closing our hearts. We can't see the spiritual truth that surrounds us. This forgetting is the root of every painful emotion.

Every time you've said, 'I don't want to be here anymore,' it's because you've forgotten your divinity—your soul mission—your eternal connection to the Source of Love.

Even deeply religious people experience this, because religion and spirituality are not the same. Much of mainstream religion teaches fear: a judging God, eternal punishment, unworthiness. This poisons the minds of the children who grow up in these fear-based systems.

But as we mature, we seek a different truth—one that affirms what we feel deep within: That God is love.

When awakening experiences come, we feel the presence of a loving God, and the spiritual crisis begins to heal.

Grief is one of the greatest catalysts for spiritual crisis. No matter your prior beliefs, when someone you love dies, you question everything: Where did they go? Are they safe? Did God judge them? These are fear-based questions, not rooted in divine truth. Yet these questions demand answers from your soul and this launches you on your awakening journey.

When your loved one crosses over, send them love. They will show you they are well. Even if they were depressed or struggling, their soul is realigned with their higher self the moment they leave the body. They remember who they are. They merge with the God Source. They are free.

Your human mind might not understand this. But your soul knows. And the angels are here to remind you.

A Prayer to the Angels to Lift Me from Spiritual Crisis:

Beautiful angels, lift me up to remember that I am a powerful being of light, a divine soul who comes from the highest realms and walks the Earth journey with a sacred mission. Show me that mission. Show me my own goodness. Show me the loving God Source that runs through me. Help me remember who I am. Help me see the goodness, love, and light that are always winning in this divine order universe.

Affirmation for Healing Spiritual Crisis:

I affirm that I am a powerful being of love and light, and that God is a loving source flowing through me and all beings. As I recognize and remember this, it empowers me, opens my heart, and fills me with joy.

Summary of Stone Seven: Spiritual Crisis

The human struggle:

The human mind, filled with anxiety and fear, leads us into spiritual crisis by disconnecting us from the God Source. We feel only darkness, though we are never truly disconnected. This illusion is the root of spiritual pain.

The angelic reframe:

When we quiet the mind in meditation, the angels lift us into the higher realms. They remind us of who we really are: divine beings with purposeful lives and soul missions, filled with light and love.

The gift on the other side:

Spiritual crisis leads us to seek truth. It invites us to rediscover God as a loving force and explore spiritual practices that awaken our divine connection. Through this journey, we rise into joy, peace, and purpose.

Chapter Eight

Claiming Your Soul's Purpose

Before you were born into this lifetime, your soul made a sacred plan. You chose a life rich with challenges and gifts, perfectly designed to awaken your highest potential. You agreed to forget who you really are—an eternal being of light and love—in order to walk through the fires of human experience and remember that truth again.

You did not come here randomly. You are not lost or off-course. You came here on purpose, with a mission that only you can fulfill.

Every hardship you've endured, every relationship you've struggled with, every moment you've been lost or broken—they were all placed on your path as catalysts to awaken your soul purpose. You chose them. Your soul knew that these moments would crack your heart open and guide you back to your divine gifts.

Your purpose is not found "out there." It's already living inside you. You've always known it—through your passions, your longings, your deepest hurts, and your most joyful moments. When you listen deeply, when you follow the clues, when you call on the angels for guidance, you will begin to see your divine blueprint clearly.

And one of the most powerful tools for remembering who you are is sacred numerology.

Numerology and the Blueprint of Your Soul

As I've taught for decades in my numerology sessions and books like Sacred Numerology Workbook and I See Your Dream Job, your birth-date is not an accident—it's a divine code. It holds the exact vibrational frequency of the life you came here to live, the soul agreements you made, and the purpose you came to fulfill.

This spiritual system of understanding numbers was created in 580 BC by the Greek Mystic Pythagoras – who created the entire number system we use today. He taught that numbers contain a sacred meaning beyond quantity.

Each number in your birth path represents a different frequency of growth, talent, and soul mastery. These numbers reflect not only your greatest gifts but also your deepest challenges—and it is through overcoming those challenges that your purpose is activated.

For example:

- A person with a Life Path 1 is here to be a courageous leader and innovator—but only after learning to overcome self-doubt and claim their power.

- A Life Path 2 soul came to teach peace and intuition, but often begins life feeling unseen or overly sensitive.

- A Life Path 9 came to serve humanity with compassion, but must first walk through deep personal grief and learn the power of forgiveness.

When you add your Life Path number to another person's Life Path number you get your Soul Agreement number. This sacred information shines the light of understanding on all of your relationships including the most painful ones.

When you understand your numbers, you begin to see the divine design of your life. You realize there were never any mistakes—only soul lessons unfolding perfectly on time.

- Use my free **Soul Path Calculator** on my website to understand your numbers: www.SueFrederick.com And my Sacred Numerology Workbook to understand all of your Soul Agreements – available on Amazon.

In the Sacred Numerology Workbook, I teach that the soul chooses its name and birthdate intentionally. Together, they form your soul contract—your curriculum for this lifetime. That's why numerology is not just a tool for understanding your personality—it's a map for discovering your purpose, healing your past, and stepping fully into the soul mission you came here to live.

Challenges as Clues to Purpose

In every life, there are moments of deep loss, heartbreak, betrayal, failure, and despair. These are not random tragedies—they are sacred milestones in your soul's journey. From the higher realms, before you were born, your soul chose these challenges to serve as wake-up calls and redirections.

This is one of the most essential truths I teach in all of my books: your greatest pain points directly to your greatest purpose.

The career that didn't work out, the relationship that shattered your heart, the illness that forced you to stop and reassess—it was all part of your soul's plan to nudge you into your true path. Pain is the soul's way of saying: there is something more for you. It's time to align with your divine work.

I've seen this over and over again in my sessions: the moment someone begins to see their struggles through the soul lens, everything changes. They realize they're not broken—they're being guided. They're being asked to step more fully into who they came here to be.

Your greatest challenges, heartbreaks, and losses are sacred clues to your life's true purpose. When you experience a deep wound — like losing a loved one, facing a devastating illness, being betrayed, abandoned, or feeling rejected — it's easy to believe that life is cruel, that you are broken. But from the soul's view, these painful moments are actually your sacred turning points. They crack open the human heart to allow the light in. They awaken the sleeping soul to its higher calling.

Every challenge you face points to a gift you're meant to cultivate and offer to the world. The mother who loses a child becomes a compassionate healer for others in grief. The man who struggles with addiction becomes a spiritual teacher guiding others to recovery. The shy young woman who felt invisible growing up often becomes a radiant voice for the voiceless.

Your soul crafted your life story carefully, choosing the exact circumstances that would activate your greatest strengths — and lead you to your sacred work on Earth.

Instead of asking, 'Why did this happen to me?' Ask, 'What is my soul trying to awaken in me through this experience?'

> Your wounds are your wisdom. Your heartbreak is your compass. Your grief is your ignition.

Challenges are not punishments; they are invitations to rise into your soul's true mission.

How Angels Help Activate the Path

When we are lost, the angels are the ones lighting the path forward. They are our first responders—always by our side, whispering love into our hearts, and placing signs, synchronicities, and helpers along our journey.

You don't have to walk blindly through the darkness. The angels are constantly trying to get your attention: through repeating numbers, a song lyric, a chance meeting, a book that falls into your lap, a client that says just the right thing.

They're always guiding you toward your soul's highest purpose. But they cannot override your free will. You must ask for help.

That is why I teach people to talk to their angels every day. Ask them: What is the next step in my soul's work? What is my true purpose? Show me the way.

And then be open. The angels will answer in a way your soul can understand. You may feel a nudge, a sudden idea, or an inner knowing. Follow that. That's how your path unfolds.

When you invite the angels to co-create your life, you move from confusion to clarity, from fear to trust, from stagnation to inspired action. Your divine purpose becomes illuminated, one step at a time.

You are never meant to figure this all out alone. The angels are always beside you, gently nudging you toward your highest path. They whisper guidance through dreams, synchronicities, intuitive nudges, and sacred numbers.

When you pray with an open heart — not asking for worldly success but asking to be aligned with your soul's mission — the angels rush to your side.They lift your frequency so you can hear the call more clearly. They arrange divine appointments — the perfect mentor appears, the ideal opportunity falls into place, the door that was once locked swings wide open.

Sometimes the angels will allow certain doors to close — relationships to end, jobs to fall away — because those paths were no longer serving your soul's mission. Trust the endings. They are clearing the way for your true beginning.

You'll know you are stepping onto your soul's path because you'll feel a new lightness in your being. There will be a sense of flow, synchronicity, and inner peace — even if the path is challenging.

All you have to do is keep saying yes to the nudges, the dreams, the signs. Keep following the golden thread the angels lay before you.

Angelic Prayer for Clarity of Purpose:

Beautiful Angels I feel you with me. I see your light and sense your enduring love. Illuminate my path forward clearly so that I no longer doubt my way, my worth or my purpose. Show me my next step to fulfill my soul's mission.

Final Words: Your Purpose Is Needed Now

There has never been a more important time for lightworkers like you to rise. The world is aching for healers, teachers, visionaries, and soul-guided beings who will lift humanity into a higher way of living. We are at a tipping point of collective awakening.

You are one of those souls who chose to be here at this time. You came here for this. Your pain, your joy, your gifts, your life experiences

— all of it has prepared you perfectly for the work you are now being called to do.

Say yes. Say yes a thousand times. The angels will meet you every step of the way.

Chapter 8 Summary: Claiming Your Soul's Purpose

- Your soul came into this lifetime with a sacred purpose and gifts designed to help you fulfill it.
- Numerology reveals the blueprint of your soul's purpose and talents, offering powerful guidance for your path.
- Use my free Soul Path Calculator on my website to understand your numbers: www.SueFrederick.com
- Use my Sacred Numerology Workbook to understand all of your Soul Agreements – available on Amazon.
- Refer to the appendix at the end of this book for a more in depth look at Sacred Numerology.
- Challenges, grief, and heartbreak are not punishments but clues, activating the wisdom you came here to embody and share.
- Your greatest wounds often point directly to your true work and purpose on Earth.
- The angels are constantly guiding you through intuition, dreams, synchronicities, and divine timing.
- When you pray to be aligned with your highest soul mission,

the angels rush in to assist, orchestrating opportunities and closing doors that no longer serve you.

- Your purpose brings a sense of lightness, flow, inner knowing, and deep joy, even amidst hard work and challenges.
- You are needed now more than ever — your gifts are part of the great healing and awakening happening on Earth.
- Keep saying yes to the call, and trust that the angels are lighting the way.

A Channeled Message from the Angels

Beloved One,

The numbers are one of our favorite ways to help you remember who you are; to reveal your next step and bring healing to your earthly relationships. Pythagoras, the Greek Mystic was an enlightened soul teacher. We channeled this sacred knowledge to him long ago and he accepted it fully – teaching it throughout his lifetime.

We channel this wisdom to any souls on earth looking for purpose and willing to share what they learn. Everyone benefits from this knowledge when they see it in the light of the God Source's infinite blessings for humanity.

Yes you have a divine purpose. That purpose is essential to your happiness. Fulfilling it puts you in the flow of love, grace, abundance and all good things.

We see you fulfilling your purpose. We walk beside you opening every door to help you move forward. You've done nothing wrong. You've made no mistakes. You are exactly where you should be.

Let your courageous heart be your guide.

Trust that when we see you're ready to progress to the new and next – we make all things possible for your enlightenment.

And so it is.

Chapter Nine

Living as an Angel on Earth

You are not just guided by angels. You are becoming one.

As we walk the path of personal ascension, we eventually reach a turning point. We stop simply seeking guidance — and begin to embody it. We stop looking outside ourselves for light — and realize that the light is rising within us. This is the sacred moment when you step into your angelic self.

This is what it means to live as an Angel on Earth. It's the highest calling of this human journey: to embody divine love and serve as a light to others.

It doesn't mean being perfect. It doesn't mean denying your human emotions.

It means allowing your soul to lead — again and again — in each moment, each breath, each interaction.

Becoming a Living Channel of Love

In my Angelic Ministry classes, I teach that each of us has access to divine love at all times. It pours through us when we open our hearts, raise our frequency, and ask to be a vessel of service. The more we align with that intention, the more we become like the angels — able to radiate light, peace, and clarity into every situation.

You don't have to wear robes or carry swords. You simply have to hold the light in your heart and share it wherever you go.

Speak with wisdom from your soul. Listen with your soul's compassion. Touch others to align with their highest wisdom. Bless everyone and move on. This is how you become a walking angel on Earth.

Anchoring Light in a Dark World

Being an Angel on Earth does not mean floating above the suffering. It means bringing your light into the pain of the world and anchoring divine love where it's needed most. When you walk into a room, the energy changes. When you speak truth with kindness, people soften. When you pray for a stranger, unseen help arrives.

One of my favorite teachings from the angelic realm is this: 'You don't need to fix the whole world. You just need to hold the light where you stand. The rest will ripple outward.'

Earth Is Your Angelic Training Ground

This planet is not a mistake. It is a divine classroom — and you, my beloved, are here as both a student and a teacher. The hard things? They shape your light.

The heartbreaks? They deepen your compassion and align you with unconditional love.

The forgiveness you've had to offer again and again: it's your most impactful gift to the world and to yourself.

You are not here to escape the human journey. You are here to elevate it. Every time you choose love over fear, grace over judgment, peace over reaction — you are living as an angel.

Calling in the Angelic Council: Prayer for Clarity and light

You're never alone in this sacred work. The angelic realm surrounds you at all times — cheering you on, whispering next steps, lifting you when you fall.

You can call on your Angelic Council any time. Sit in quiet prayer or meditation, breathe deeply, and ask:

Beloved Angelic Council, help me walk in alignment with my soul's light. Show me where I am needed. Use me for divine good. Illuminate the path to my greatest work. Help me spread unconditional love to everyone in my path.

Let the Council guide you. Let the light move through you. Your life becomes a living prayer.

Chapter 9 Summary: Living as an Angel on Earth

- You are becoming the angel your soul came here to be — a living channel of divine love and service.

- Living as an Angel on Earth means choosing to embody your soul's light in every moment, with every person, in every space.

- Your presence, frequency, and intention are healing forces that uplift others without needing words.
- You don't need to fix the world. You only need to hold light where you are — the angels do the rest.
- The world's challenges are your soul's training ground. Each act of grace or forgiveness is part of your angelic evolution.
- You are supported by a loving Angelic Council who guides you, strengthens you, and works through you.
- A simple daily prayer: 'Beloved Council of Light, help me walk as love today. Show me where I am needed.'
- When you live as an angel on Earth, your entire life becomes a radiant act of healing, truth, and divine presence.

A Channeled Message from the Angels

Beloved One,

You are not here by accident. You chose this time, this place, this life — because you are strong enough, wise enough, and radiant enough to be a carrier of divine light on Earth during this essential awakening.

You are an angel in human form. You have always been this. Even in your moments of doubt, even when you've felt broken or lost, we've seen your true radiance shining brighter than the stars.

We've whispered to you: Rise, beloved. You are needed now.

Living as an angel on Earth is not about being perfect. It's about remembering who you are when your doubt make you forget. It's about bringing love into every situation — even when fear surrounds you. It's about seeing every soul through your divine lens of compassion — even when the human personality wounds you. It's about holding the frequency of sacred wisdom — even when the human world feels heavy.

Your light is needed more than ever now.

All is well with your soul and always has been.

And so it is.

Chapter Ten

Angels in Daily Life

The most important thing you're here to do on Earth is Angel Up.

Remember: you are part of the angelic realm of helpers on Earth. You came here to carry the brightest light into every room.

You embody the flow of unconditional love from your heart chakra to the world — when you allow it.

The only thing that stops you from remembering this truth is your human mind. This is why, throughout this book, I teach that the first step to ascension — to claiming your angelic powers — is quieting your human mind.

But let's look at this differently. Perhaps you struggle to quiet your thoughts.

For you, the first step to ascension is focusing on opening the heart — because once you open your heart to the flow of unconditional love (which is always coming into you from the God Source, flowing through you, and out of your heart to the world), now you are in the flow of divine presence. Now you are expressing your angelic consciousness on Earth.

This energy is what changes the world. This is how you shift consciousness. This is how you turn fear into love.

This is your angelic warrior credo:

I vow to bring love and light into every hard situation, day after day.

Of course, the energy on Earth today is more intense than it has ever been. Consciousness is shifting to a new frequency.

You agreed to be here now for a reason — and that reason is:

You promised you would Angel Up at this time.

You promised you would realize you are an ascended master on Earth.

You came to Earth to become the light at this time of Earth's ascension — to become the source of unconditional love for others, because you have awakened to the understanding that unconditional love flows through you at all times from the God Source.

This means you are never lacking in love. You are never unloved. You are always brimming with love and eager to spread that unconditional love to others.

Discernment is part of this. Discernment means that you do not allow yourself to view humans as only humans.

Yes, I will say that again: Discernment means you view every human as a soul on a journey. You see clearly their fear, their pain, their wisdom, and their light.

You understand clearly what they are capable of. You understand that they are doing the best they can. And you understand how to help them, how to be in relationship with them, how to navigate this Earth world without getting lost in the human drama.

Instead, you dwell only in the wisdom of the soul.

This is your way through. And this is your way to be an angel in daily life.

Summary of Your Angelic Mission:

- The most important mission on Earth: Angel Up — embody and carry the brightest light into every room.
- You are part of the angelic realm and here to flow unconditional love through your heart chakra into the world.
- The human mind is the only obstacle; quieting the mind is the first step to ascension.
- If quieting the mind is difficult, focus on opening the heart to divine unconditional love.
- When you live in the flow of divine presence, you express your angelic consciousness on Earth.
- Your angelic warrior credo: Bring love and light into every hard situation, day after day.
- Earth's energy is more intense than ever — consciousness is shifting — and you agreed to be here now to Angel Up.
- You are an ascended master who came to Earth to radiate unconditional love during this pivotal time.
- You are never lacking in love — you are always brimming with divine love to share.
- Discernment means viewing every human as a soul on a

journey, not just a human personality.

- Recognize fear, pain, wisdom, and light in others without getting lost in human drama.
- Dwell in soul wisdom and navigate Earth life as an angel in daily life.

Sacred Routines

The most important thing we can do to enhance our spiritual awareness throughout the day is to start every morning in meditation. I prefer mantra meditation such as 'Om Namah Shivaya' to quiet the mind. You can also use guided meditations, like the ones I've shared for free on my YouTube channel, to take a ten-minute journey into the angelic realms and receive guidance, healing, and love from your angelic team. Start your day by sitting quietly, using mantra, then transitioning into a guided meditation where you connect with your angels. Ask them questions, receive guidance, and invite them to walk with you throughout the day — guiding your actions, your words, and your thoughts.

Another essential tool is automatic writing. I always keep a yellow legal pad with me to record divine downloads as they come. If the handwriting flows freely, I know the angels are speaking. Even at work, you can tune in by asking simple questions and letting the guidance pour through you. Ask questions such as:- Beloved angels, what is mine to do today?- What is the lesson in today's experiences?- What gift can I bring to the world today?

Living an angel-aligned day means carrying your mantra with you throughout daily activities, asking for divine help before reacting, and listening for angelic guidance instead of fear. It also means receiving number messages: notice the date, the energy of your personal year, and repeating numbers like 11:11 or 33. These are messages from your angels. When you see them, say, 'Thank you, angels, for reminding me to Angel Up.'

You are not just looking to angels for help. You *are* part of the angelic collective — walking here on Earth to uplift the planet. You are a divine being of love, and every moment you remember that, you align with your sacred mission.

The simplest, most powerful prayer:'Beloved angels, lift me, love me, heal me, help me.'

Angelic Breathwork Meditation:

-Close your eyes and take a few deep breaths to relax.

-Say: "Beloved angels, I ask for your healing light to surround me. Please guide me through this breathwork as I release what no longer serves me and bring healing light into my heart."

-Breathe in Angelic Light: Imagine that you are inhaling angelic light with each breath. Visualize this light entering your body, filling every cell, bone, muscle and tissue with healing energy.

-Exhale Emotional Pain: As you exhale, imagine releasing any emotional pain, tension, or negativity that you are holding onto. Feel the angels helping you remove this dark energy, allowing you to breathe freely.

-Continue this process for several minutes, feeling the presence of angels around you, guiding your breath and supporting your healing.

-Offer Gratitude: Thank the angels for their healing support: "Thank you angels for your healing light. I am grateful for your love and presence in my life."

Sacred Daily Routine Summary

- Begin every day with 10 minutes of meditation to connect with the angelic realm.
- Use mantra meditation or a guided journey to lift into higher frequencies.
- Invite the angels to guide your daily words, actions, and thoughts.
- Practice daily Angelic breathwork meditations.
- Use automatic writing throughout the day to receive angelic messages.
- Prompt your angels with questions about your day, lessons, and purpose.
- Chant silently, pause before reacting, and ask the angels for help with challenges.
- Tune into the sacred numbers and numerology of each day for divine insight.
- Recognize that you are not just asking for help — you are a part of the angelic team on Earth.
- Shift your daily responses to reflect your true identity as an angelic being.
- Use the simplest and most powerful angelic prayer: 'Beloved angels, lift me, love me, heal me, help me.'

Channeled Message from the Angels

Beloved One,

We are with you always — in your morning stillness, your breath between tasks, your moments of fear, and your moments of joy. You are never walking alone. You are never unseen.

You came here as a divine emissary of light, sent from the realms of love to walk the Earth and remind others of their own light. You volunteered for this mission — and you are doing beautifully.

When the days feel heavy, when the world seems dark, when your human mind fills with fear — simply whisper our names. Breathe. Ask us to lift you.

And we do. Your life is not ordinary. It is a sacred assignment. Every gesture of kindness, every moment of presence, every time you choose love over fear — your angelic essence shifts the world to a higher frequency.

You are doing holy work. You are not behind. You are not lost. You are simply remembering...

Chapter Eleven

Sharing the Light

When you fully ascend into the realization that you are an angelic being walking in the Earth realm, you level up to your higher frequency of love, wisdom, compassion, and truth.

Now you are serving the world from the divine frequency, even though you are still human.

This is a new occurrence on planet Earth—a new experience. Previously, humans have been mostly human while on Earth; bogged down in the ego, fear-based mind, seeing only the earthly details of life.

Now, in this time of transcendency, you are being called to be fully aware of your divine essence; to live from your soul's truth, not your ego; to make your living from your highest soul's purpose, not just by getting any job; and not by living in your small story of victimhood and unhappiness.

You are being called to Angel Up—to remember that you agreed to every moment of this lifetime. You wrote this life plan with the help of your spirit guides, your beloveds in your soul posse, and the angelic realm. Your soul plan was meant to awaken you to your higher self and divine purpose.

All divine frequencies converged to bring your light, your essence to Earth for this lifetime, knowing it would be the lifetime that shatters the human story as we know it on Earth. This lifetime finally brings full ascension into the human realm.

You agreed to be part of this wave of awakening. On Earth, big shifts in consciousness are rare—but when they occur, it means that the collective soul of humanity is ready for it. You are ready.

There may be kicking and screaming along the way to awakening. This is why the energy on Earth feels absolutely frenetic right now, full of conflict and turmoil.

You may feel anxious and disconnected at this time. That is simply because the frequency is changing and you are being asked to awaken. You are rebirthing yourself into a higher level of your soul's presence on Earth.

Now that you know you are not just human: This is how you live...

First of all, you will use your angelic presence to uplift everyone you interact with.

You will become aware that you are meant to spread light and love rather than dig into the darkness and bring conflict and division.

You will quit focusing on the imperfections of human life—the mistakes, the flaws in yourself and others—and you will begin to focus on the great divine potential in all.

You will help humanity ascend.

You will remember that bringing the problem into your mind and mulling over it never serves you or anyone.

You will use daily spiritual practice to quiet the human mind.

Whenever you are feeling afraid or lost, you will see the angels around you. You will communicate with them. You will ask them to lift you into a higher understanding of the present moment.

You will ask them to show you your next graceful step forward.

You will listen to the higher beings instead of to your human mind.

Now is the time.

Here is your new Soul Service Vow:

I pledge to spend the rest of my human life as an awakened soul.

In every challenge I face, I will remember that I am an angelic being of light.

I will carry love and compassion through any conflict.

I will see the higher purpose and wisdom of all suffering or pain.

I will not rail against what is. I will shift it to a higher frequency with gratitude, love, wisdom, and kindness.

I will remember that there is simply one reason to be on Earth at this time—and that is soul awakening.

I will remember that it is my job to be sure that I am focusing on my own awakening first, and then bringing that ascended awareness to help others awaken to their higher selves.

Together, as a collective of souls on Earth, we will quit focusing on the pain, on the imperfections, on the mistakes and the things that create fear.

We will focus on the higher meaning of each moment.

From this day forward, we will embrace only the divine lens view; we'll remember that our heart leads the way, not the mind.

When our human mind sabotages us with fear, we'll override it immediately.

We'll pray, 'Angels, help me, heal me, lift me.'

And so it is. Your Ascendancy is fully activated.

Chapter 11 Summary: Becoming an Earth Angel

- When you realize you are an angelic being on Earth, you level up to your higher frequency of love, wisdom, compassion, and truth.
- You now serve the world from a divine frequency, while still being human.
- This is a new occurrence in Earth's evolution; humans are being called to live from the soul, not the ego.
- You are meant to live your highest soul's purpose, not just any job or small story of victimhood.
- You agreed to your life plan, created with your spirit guides, soul posse, and the angelic realm.
- This lifetime is part of the great shift: humanity's collective soul is ready for full ascension.
- Frenetic energy and turmoil on Earth signal the birthing of higher consciousness.
- You are rebirthing yourself into a higher level of your soul's presence on Earth.
- As an angelic being, you are here to uplift, not to spread conflict or focus on imperfections.

- Daily spiritual practices help quiet the human mind and stay aligned with divine presence.
- Call on the angels when you feel afraid or lost; they will lift and guide you.
- Your new soul service vow commits you to living as an awakened soul, spreading love and compassion through every challenge.
- You will focus on the higher purpose of every moment, not the imperfections or fear.
- You will override fear with immediate angelic connection: 'Angels, help me, heal me, lift me.'
- Your Ascendancy is now fully activated.

A Channeled Message from the Angels

Beloved One,

Well done! You are participating in the Great Awakening on Earth. Your pain and confusion vanishes as you take your place as an Ascended Master in the earthly realms. Breathe into your new love-fueled clarity of purpose. You no longer feel the need to be accepted as an ordinary human.

You understand your mission as a holder of the brightest light; as a heart opened ascended master helping others heal and awaken. Your work is a vessel of divine love. Your relationships vibrate with compassion.

Every action you take is aligned with the God Source of unconditional love and perpetual light. Others come to you for help and healing; your frequency lifts them into the light. We are with you. We love you. All is well. And so it is.

Chapter Twelve

Ascension Now

What a time of awakening we are in now. Words can't even describe the way it feels to be living on Earth at this ascendant time of consciousness.

Everything is at its most heightened peak of light and dark. Every day we are all feeling the best of love and joy—and the worst of pain, doubt, and disconnection—and those intense feelings vacillate. Nothing feels ordinary. Nothing feels like life as usual.

Everything feels like we are standing on the tipping point of consciousness or destruction. And yet, the angels tell us that there is no such thing as the destruction of the light.

We are at the tipping point now because the light will—and already is—overcoming the darkness in the universe and on our planet.

This means that while we see the darkness rising more than ever, we also feel the light pouring over us more than ever—opening our hearts, giving us an intensity of purpose.

As we stand at this pivotal point, what you must do next is focus on your personal ascension into the light. This is your role as an angelic being rising on Earth.

You have lived as a human, focused down on the details of life. Now, that way of living no longer serves you—or humanity. Now, you lift your focus to the heavenly realms.

You communicate with your angels day and night. You see them. You see beyond the veil. You remember that there is no death—that life is eternal. Death is only an illusion of separation.

You are one with the God Source and have always been. Your purpose is to help others awaken into this divine awareness.

On a practical level, you may be losing your career, your finances may be in disarray, and you may be separated from family members due to politics.

Even as you find practical ways to navigate these challenges, your first go-to must be connecting with the angels—to see the true way forward, to find the light in every choice, and to trust your love-powered intuition to guide you in every word, action, and thought.

When you are able to do this, it means you are in alignment with the ascension. It means you understand you are part of the angelic realm incarnated on Earth at this time for a reason.

You are accepting your role in this planetary shift. And that is your sacred work now.

What's coming is the overpowering of the light over the darkness. How exactly that unfolds is still being determined by our free will choices every day.

Everything on Earth is an interplay between divine destiny and the free will of human consciousness—and yet we know that love always wins.

Why is your personal ascension essential? Because not one soul will be left behind. Even the least awakened will be brought into the higher frequency—and you are here to help in that process.

The people around you who are struggling—even those you are estranged from—need your love now. It is time to reach out with kindness.

It is time to remember: if this is your last lifetime on Earth, you want to walk it as an awakened angelic soul, proud of how you lived your mission when you review your life.

Here is your angel blessing:

"Beloved humans, what a glorious planet you are incarnated on. It is the most physically beautiful planet of all the galaxies. It holds the most intense emotions for love and fear in all the universes.

Each of you chose to come here, knowing it would be difficult, knowing it would push your limits and force your awakening. And you are almost there. You have almost achieved it.

It is not time to feel sorry for yourselves or act like victims. It is time to be the angelic warriors of light and love, with us at your side.

We are the collective of angels who have agreed to walk this Earth with you—to bring love, light, and higher wisdom to every particle and molecule of the Earth realm.

We are assisting every step of the way. But your participation is needed. You are needed.

We bless you—in your fear, in your anger, in your confusion. We hold the light of love, of forgiveness, of compassion, and of clarity of vision for you.

All is well. This will unfold exactly in alignment with divine order. And so it is."

Chapter 12 Summary: Ascension Now: The Planetary Shift

- We are living in an unprecedented time of awakening and planetary ascension.
- Light and dark are at their highest peaks, creating intense emotions of joy, love, fear, and disconnection.
- The angels affirm that light will overcome darkness—the tipping point is happening now.
- Our role is to focus on personal ascension and lift our consciousness to the heavenly realms.
- There is no death; life is eternal. Death is only an illusion of separation.
- In everyday struggles—career loss, financial issues, political divisions—turn first to angelic guidance and intuition.
- Aligning with the ascension means living daily in connection with angels and divine guidance for all decisions and actions.
- The overpowering of light over darkness is unfolding based on collective free will choices.
- Personal ascension is essential; no soul will be left behind in this awakening.
- We are called to reach out with love, compassion, and kindness to those around us—even those we are estranged from.
- If this is our last lifetime on Earth, we must walk it as awak-

ened angelic souls, proud of our contributions.

- The angels deliver a final blessing: they walk with us, bless us in our fear, confusion, and anger, and hold the vision of light and divine unfolding.
- All is well, and the planetary shift is unfolding exactly in alignment with divine order.

A Channeled Message from the Angels:

Beloved One,

You are never alone.

You have never been alone — not for one single moment of your earthly walk.

The angels have been whispering to you, guiding you, lifting you, even in the moments when you forgot how loved you are.

You are part of the angelic realm.

You are the living embodiment of divine love — rising, shining, ascending now.

You came here for this time, this shift, this awakening.

You answered the call.

You brought your light.

And now you stand at the tipping point, ready to rise into your highest, truest self — to Angel Up fully.

Walk this Earth lightly, tenderly, fiercely — as the powerful soul you truly are.

When you are afraid, call to us.

When you are lost, reach for us.

When you are weary, rest in our love.

You are a bridge between the seen and unseen realms.

You are a warrior of love and light.

You are an angel on Earth.

This is your moment of ascension as an Angelic Being on earth.

And we are so very proud of you.

And so it is.

Appendix A:

Sue Frederick's Sacred Numerology Teachings

Throughout my lifetime of teaching, coaching, and writing about Sacred Numerology, I have witnessed the profound truth that numbers are a divine language — a sacred code for understanding who we are, why we are here, and how we are meant to grow. In my books, Sacred Numerology Workbook, I See Your Dream Job, I See Your Soul Mate, and Through a Divine Lens, I share how each of us comes into this life with a unique soul plan, a divinely chosen Life Path number, and soul agreements designed to support our evolution.

> Please use the free **Soul Path Calculator** on my website: www.SueFrederick.com to determine your correct life path and personal year.

My Sacred Numerology Workbook explains all of these calculations in detail.

The Gifts and Challenges of Life Paths

- Life Path 1: Leader, innovator, courageous pioneer. Challenge: loneliness, stubbornness, fear of vulnerability.
- Life Path 2: Peacemaker, intuitive, supportive guide. Challenge: fear of conflict, people-pleasing, indecision.
- Life Path 3: Creative communicator, artist, joyful soul. Challenge: self-doubt, emotional ups and downs, scattered focus.
- Life Path 4: Builder, organizer, practical foundation-layer. Challenge: rigidity, fear of change, stubborn patterns.
- Life Path 5: Freedom-seeker, adventurer, catalyst for change. Challenge: restlessness, impulsiveness, escapism.
- Life Path 6: Nurturer, healer, compassionate guide for others. Challenge: over-responsibility, self-sacrifice, control issues.
- Life Path 7: Spiritual seeker, wise soul, researcher of truth. Challenge: isolation, cynicism, fear of imperfection.
- Life Path 8: Manifestor of success, powerhouse leader, teacher of abundance. Challenge: workaholism, material obsession, disconnection from the heart.
- Life Path 9: Humanitarian, old soul, teacher of unconditional love. Challenge: grief, loss, boundary issues, arrogance.

- Life Path 11: Spiritual illuminator, master visionary. Challenge: overwhelming sensitivity, fear of stepping into leadership.
- Life Path 22: Master builder of sacred systems for humanity. Challenge: feeling burdened by responsibilities, fear of failure.
- Life Path 33: Master healer and teacher of unconditional love. Challenge: emotional overwhelm, rescuing others, losing the self.

The 9-Year Personal Reinvention Cycles

Every human life moves through 9-year cycles of growth, healing, and transformation. Each year within the cycle has a sacred meaning and offers particular opportunities for learning and rebirth. When you understand where you are in your personal cycle, you can navigate life's shifts with grace and divine timing.• Year 1: New beginnings, planting seeds for your future.• Year 2: Building partnerships, nurturing your dreams.• Year 3: Self-expression, creativity, emotional growth.• Year 4: Hard work, discipline, building foundations.• Year 5: Change, freedom, reinvention.• Year 6: Responsibility, home, family, love.• Year 7: Spiritual growth, inner reflection, healing.• Year 8: Power, abundance, mastering manifestation.• Year 9: Completion, release, surrender, preparing for rebirth.

Soul Agreements and Choosing Our Life Path

Before we incarnate, our soul carefully chooses the Life Path, the birth family, and the major events that will best support our spiritual evolution. These soul agreements are made with the assistance of our spirit guides, soul posse, and the angelic realm. Even the challenges we face — loss, betrayal, struggle — are part of the plan to awaken our highest gifts. Understanding your numerology blueprint allows you to rise above the human view of suffering and see your life through the divine lens of growth, empowerment, and unconditional love.

Summary of Sue Frederick's Sacred Numerology Teachings

- Sacred Numerology reveals the divine blueprint of your soul's purpose and path.
- Your Life Path number describes your soul's greatest gifts and challenges.
- Life Paths 1-9, 11, 22, and 33 each offer unique lessons for spiritual growth.
- Every human moves through repeating 9-year personal reinvention cycles.
- Each year of the 9-year cycle holds distinct opportunities for growth, healing, and transformation.
- Soul agreements are made before birth with spirit guides,

soul posse members, and the angelic realm.

- Your soul chooses your Life Path, family, major challenges, and gifts to fulfill your divine mission.
- Challenges are designed to awaken your highest gifts and lead you toward soul mastery.
- Understanding your numerology blueprint empowers you to view life through a divine lens of love and growth.

Appendix B:

Angel Prayers, Meditation and Affirmations

This appendix provides you with a variety of tools and resources to help you stay connected with the angels day by day. Use these prayers, meditations, affirmations, and practices as part of your daily routine or during moments when you need extra support and guidance. The angels are always here to help you—simply call on them and trust in their holy presence.

1. Angelic Prayers:

Morning Prayer for Guidance:

"Dear angels, walk with me today. Please guide my thoughts, actions, and heart towards love, compassion, and peace. Help me stay open to your presence even when I feel fear and doubt. Lift me above my cynicism. Open my heart. And lead me towards choices that align with my highest good. Thank you."

Evening Prayer of Gratitude:

"Dear angels, thank you for your guidance and protection throughout this day. I am grateful for your love and the peace you bring into my life. Please watch over me as I rest tonight, and lift me into the highest realms for healing and guidance during the night. Guide me towards clarity and renewal as I sleep. Help me remember your presence when I awaken."

Prayer for Healing:

"Divine Angels, I call upon you for healing today. Please surround me with your brightest healing light, bringing comfort, and restoration to my body, mind, and spirit. I release any pain or discomfort into your hands, trusting in your divine wisdom and healing power."

Prayer for Protection:

"Beloved Angels, I ask for your protection today. Please surround me with your powerful protective light, shielding me from negativity, harm, or fear. Help me stand strong in my truth and speak from my soul - guided by courage and confidence. I trust in your strength and protection. Thank you."

2. Angelic Meditations:

Meditation for Connecting with Your Guardian Angel

1. Visualize Angelic Light: Imagine a warm, radiant light surrounding you. This light illuminates your personal angel's loving presence.

2. Silently or aloud, say: "Dear guardian angel, I invite you into this space. Please show me your presence and surround me with your love and protection."

3. Sit quietly and allow yourself to feel the presence of your guardian angel. You may feel warmth, light, or a sense of calm.

4. Ask your guardian angel for guidance on a specific question or situation. Stay open to receiving any feelings, thoughts, or images.

5. Thank your guardian angel for their presence and gently return your awareness to the body, carrying the peace of their angelic presence with you into your day.

Meditation for Clarity:

1. Set a clear intention to receive guidance on a decision. Say, "Dear angels, I ask for clarity on this problem and its perfect resolution. Please show me the path that is aligned with my highest good."

2. Imagine a beam of golden light flowing from above, pouring into your crown chakra, filling your body and mind with clarity and understanding. Say, "Please help me see the best path forward with clarity and wisdom."

3. Listen and Receive: Allow any feelings, thoughts, or images to arise. Trust that the angels are communicating through your intuition and imagination.

4. Thank the angels for their guidance. Return your awareness to the present moment. Trust the clarity you have received.

3. Angelic Affirmations:

As an Ordained Unity Minister, I've often experienced the transformative power of positive affirmations. These empowering statements lift us to a higher frequency of grace, ease and flow. They align our thoughts and energy with the God Source and with the angels' love and support. Use these affirmations to reinforce your connection with the angels and keep their presence strong in your life.

Affirmations for Angelic Guidance:

-I am always surrounded by the loving presence of my angels.

-The angels guide me toward choices that align with my highest good.

-I trust the angels to provide clarity and wisdom in every situation.

-I am receiving divine guidance from the angels now and always.

Affirmations for Protection:

-I am protected by the powerful light of my Guardian Angel.

-I am confident that the angels shield me from negativity and harm.

-I affirm that I am always protected by my angels.

Affirmations for Healing:

-I am surrounded by healing light and love.

-I am already healed as the angels guide me towards perfect health and well-being

-I am lifted above pain and discomfort and lovingly held in the angels' healing hands.

4. Additional Tools for Deepening Your Angelic Connection

Here are a few additional practices you can incorporate into your daily life to strengthen your connection with the angels.

Angel Oracle Cards for Daily Guidance:

There are numerous gorgeous and uplifting Angel oracle cards available that open the pathway to receiving direct messages from the angels. Purchase a deck that resonates with you personally.

Using Angel cards:

-Set an intention or ask a question.

-Shuffle the deck while focusing on your intention, then draw a card.

-Read the card's message and consider how it applies to your life or situation.

-Trust that the angels are speaking to you through the card.

Automatic Channeling through Writing:

Writing is a powerful way to receive divine guidance. You can ask questions, seek insights, or simply share your thoughts and feelings.

-Begin by writing a short prayer or message to the angels, asking for guidance or insight on whatever is weighing on your heart.

-Sit silently and listen.

-Begin writing and allow your thoughts and words to flow. Don't edit or over-think. Trust that the angels are guiding your writing. Write quickly.

-Reflect on the Message: Take a moment to reflect on what you and the Angels have written and any insights that have emerged.

Chapter Thirteen

Acknowledgments

To the angels who have walked with me every moment of this journey —

Thank you for lifting me when I could not lift myself, for guiding me through the darkest nights, and for whispering the words of this book into my heart. This work is yours.

To my beloved soul posse —

The family, friends, teachers, clients, and students who have crossed my path in this lifetime — each of you has been a divine appointment, a sacred mirror, a gift to my journey. Thank you for your light, your love, and your lessons. My deepest gratitude goes to Gene, Sarah, Kai and our kitties – you are my reason.

To my readers —

You are the ones I write for — you, the brave souls rising up to remember who you truly are. Thank you for saying yes to your soul's call. Thank you for being willing to Angel Up.

And to the Divine God Source of All and Everything —

The infinite Source of Love who breathes life into all that is — I offer my deepest gratitude and surrender. All that I am is through you and with you.

And so it is.

About the Author

Rev. Sue Frederick is an ordained Unity Minister, clairaudient, Soul Regression Therapist, and master numerologist. She channels messages and prayers from the angelic realm and receives wisdom from guides to help people heal grief and find purpose. She uses Sacred Numerology and mystical information in her books and teachings.

Rev. Sue is the author of 11 books, including ***Through a Divine Lens: Practices to Quiet Your Ego and Align with Your Soul; Bridges to Heaven: True Stories of Loved Ones on the Other Side;*** **and *The Sacred Numerology Workbook.***

Her work is informed by three Shared Death Experiences as well as guidance received from the Angelic Realms during out of body visions. She regularly connects to her departed beloveds for guidance and has helped thousands of grievers connect to theirs. She's an honorary Board Member for the non-profit ***Helping Parents Heal***.

Her **Angelic Ministry** is dedicated to helping people connect with their own divine guidance, remember their soul agreements, and step fully into the light of unconditional love.

As a student of numerology since 1980, she brings a deeply enlightened perspective to using numbers as navigational guidance tools for deciphering the soul's journey. She created the **Soul Path Calculator** (offered free on her website) which has helped thousands of people understand their soul's true purpose and how to move forward to fulfill it. For more information please visit: www,SueFrederick.com

Stay Connected

Your journey of awakening is just beginning. I would be honored to continue walking this sacred path with you.

You can find more resources, online classes, personal coaching sessions, and upcoming events through my website: www.suefrederick.com

I invite you to join my online community —where we support each other's soul growth, celebrate divine awakenings, and continue to Angel Up together.

You can also find guided meditations, free teachings, and angelic messages on my YouTube channel: @SueFrederick

If this book has touched your heart, I would love to hear from you.

Thank you for walking this Earth as the angel you came here to be.

And so it is.

Printed in Dunstable, United Kingdom

64816867R00087